"I have worked directly with Ma
cept-writing expert. In *Marketi*
have the chance to learn all th
has been sharing with clients for years."

—Wendy Warus, Vice President of Marketing,
Henkel/Dial Corporation Consumer Goods

"This highly-readable book, based on Martha's years of personal experience in many industries offers valuable background as well as helpful advice on crafting effective concepts. *Marketing Concepts That Win!* offers something for everyone—whether you are new to concept writing or need to fine-tune your existing skills."

—Praveen Kopalle, Professor of Marketing, Tuck School
of Business at Dartmouth, Dartmouth College

"A must-read for marketers . . . Using a fresh, no-nonsense, and completely approachable style, Martha walks you through each step of the concept-creation process to simplify the process and ensure that you can do it, too."

—From the foreword by Howard Moskowitz, PhD,
president of Moskowitz Jacobs, CEO of i-Novation,
and author of twenty-five books

"Martha's approach has helped us build ownable concepts for key business lines across the world. Her proven strategies for writing effective concepts keep our team focused on the key principles of building winning concepts. Consumers around the world need a reason to buy your product. You must discover and clearly articulate that reason, and with *Marketing Concepts That Win!*, you can."

—Deborah L. Asmara, Director, Global Brand Management,
Personal Care & Home Care, Amway International

Marketing Concepts That *Win!*

SAVE TIME, MONEY AND WORK BY CRAFTING CONCEPTS RIGHT THE FIRST TIME

MARTHA GUIDRY

LIVE OAK
BOOK COMPANY

Published by Live Oak Book Company
Austin, TX
www.liveoakbookcompany.com

Distributed by Live Oak Book Company

For ordering information or special discounts for bulk purchases,
please contact Live Oak Book Company at PO Box 91869, Austin, TX
78709, 512.891.6100.

Design and composition by Greenleaf Book Group LLC
and Bumpy Design
Cover design by Greenleaf Book Group LLC

Publisher's Cataloging-In-Publication Data
(Prepared by The Donohue Group, Inc.)
Guidry, Martha.
    Marketing concepts that win! : save time, money and work by crafting
concepts right the first time / Martha Guidry. — 1st ed.
    p. ; cm.
    Issued also as an ebook.
    Includes bibliographical references and index.
    ISBN: 978-1-936909-14-8

    1. Communication in marketing. 2. New products—Marketing. 3.
New products—Planning. 4. Business writing. I. Title.
HF5415.123 .G85 2011
658.802   2011935485

Print ISBN: 978-1-936909-14-8
eBook ISBN: 978-1-936909-15-5

First Edition

CONTENTS

FOREWORD

This is an important book for two reasons: It deals with a key topic in business—the concept—and it presents how to do it. Those two reasons make this book a must-read for marketers.

First, for the 'why' of this book: Business people (and even academics) need what's in this book. Simply put, if you create a good product or service and sell it, you get to keep your job, get promoted, and may even get to make a lot of money! Pretty simple, right?

Now for the gravitas: Identifying and creating a winning concept—a concept that makes the target audience get excited and desire your offering—is FUNDAMENTAL to the success of launching any product or service in the marketplace. As simple as this sounds, creating an effective, single-minded positioning concept trips up marketers and market researchers on a regular basis. They just get it wrong, time after time. And there's less and less forgiveness in today's business world for those who get it wrong.

Let's take a look at one example from the fast food

industry. The McDonald's Arch Deluxe hamburger launched with fanfare and corporate hoopla in 1996. Like every other company in the fast food world, McDonalds wanted a bigger piece of the adult business. The Deluxe line was meant to market McDonalds anew, at least to the adult demographic, as fine(r) cuisine. With this launch, kids would be happy with fast food, and their parents would finally be more satisfied with something more upscale. Unfortunately, the launch failed miserably, due to a poor positioning concept complementing a lackluster product. As it turned out, adults weren't interested in paying significantly more money for what ended up to be a marginally different burger. It is striking to me that a company with so much consumer success took such a significant misstep. They've done their homework since the Deluxe debacle. Look at McCafe, created to compete with upscale coffee companies. McCafe is incredibly successful: a competitive coffee at a compellingly competitive price.

In her practice, Martha Guidry opens up the science and art of creating winning concepts with a refreshingly different and practical approach. Martha has presented this information at conferences and trained her Fortune 500 clients in positioning concept development. Her ideas and strategies are battle tested. That's important. Even more important, Martha shares those same strategies with you, giving you an effective way to build a better concept. That's where the "beef" is.

In Martha's experience, writing brief and on-topic concepts ends up being one of the client's biggest challenges, often a daunting (and even disheartening) one. Many marketers are never formally trained to write effective concepts.

In addition, too much knowledge and too much involvement gets in the way of successful concepting. All too often, the client knows so much about his product or service offering that it ends up being difficult to select only the pieces that work, the bare-to-the-bones words that should be said. Instead, they throw in all sorts of stuff that just sits there like a lump, irrelevant and obscuring the message that needs to be communicated. And finally, there's that ubiquitous 800 pound gorilla—the committee. When writing concepts by committee (and who hasn't been in that situation), each member may have a sense of the truth. And who wants to get in the way of truth? So the concept goes on and on and on, ending up nowhere.

Marketing Concepts That Win! breaks that cycle and teaches you what the Concept Queen has been doing for over 15 years. Starting her early marketing career with the Goliath of consumer products, Procter & Gamble, Martha benefited from a firm foundation in concept development. As her career progressed and she became an independent consultant, she enhanced and refined her skills by working with a variety of clients, some in her backyard and some as far away as Shanghai, China. Martha presents a breadth of knowledge and experience in a timeless book that should be on the shelf of anyone involved in developing and writing positioning concepts—marketers, market researchers, advertising agencies, and business owners. More importantly, it should be on YOUR bookshelf. The bottom line is that you WILL benefit from her practical, clearly written guidebook.

Reflect for a minute upon the brand(s) you've been entrusted with. Maybe you've got an established product or service that is now lagging in the marketplace because it doesn't exactly speak to today's market. Maybe you've got a relatively new and innovative product or service that, in spite of its evident quality, is struggling to succeed, to connect with the consumer in a way that is clear, persuasive and profitable. Or maybe you've tried writing concepts that just haven't performed as well as you'd like. Help is on the way. *Marketing Concepts That Win!* provides a soup-to-nuts resource for concept writing. Plus, it lays out a complete game plan to follow before you even get started writing your winning concept, ensuring that you've collected all the essential information you need to do the job right. Make no mistake: anyone who has tried to write a positioning concept knows that a clear, compelling concept is surprisingly difficult to create. Using a fresh, no-nonsense, and completely approachable style, Martha walks you through each step of concept creation to simplify the process and ensure that you can do it, too.

Whether this is your first time developing a concept or you are a seasoned concept-writing professional, Martha's nuggets of information and helpful tips will truly save you time and money. My opinion: You'd be crazy not to give *Marketing Concepts That Win!* a read. You'll never know what you're missing until you give it a look!

Howard Moskowitz, Ph.D., President of Moskowitz Jacobs and CEO of i-Novation, is the author of 25 books and 400 articles and has received many awards for his contributions to psychology and market research.

PREFACE

HOW TO USE THIS BOOK

How can you best use this book? Well, that depends on your needs, where you are in your concept-development effort, what you are trying to accomplish, and your level of experience. But wherever you are, the information in this book can be helpful in a variety of situations. Let's look at a few possible scenarios.

- You are new to marketing or market research and want to learn more about what a marketing concept is and how to create one that will test well with your target audience.
- You are in new territory with your product or service and have completed a variety of research activities to understand the need gaps in your product category. You will now formulate a winning marketing concept and then go back to the "lab" to create it.
- You have already created the core product or service

and are now working to refine a positioning concept for it.

- You are creating a line extension under an existing brand that needs to have "ownable" space to separate it from the mother brand.
- You've tested concepts with lackluster results and want to understand if they were impaired by poor communication or writing.

To help prepare you, I've outlined the focus of each part of the book. If you think you are ready to jump into the how-tos of concept writing, then start with chapter 6. Otherwise, here are some areas worthy of exploration to further enhance your knowledge.

- Chapters 1–3 focus on foundational knowledge and context regarding concept development and writing. These chapters can be particularly helpful for those who are relatively new to the process, but they are also useful as a refresher for more seasoned individuals.
- Chapters 4 and 5 focus on the structure of a positioning concept and the three elements—content, relevance, and language—that need to be integrated for successful concept writing.
- Chapters 6–10 concentrate on the actual writing of the key elements in a concept—and on deciding whether an illustration or image should be used to take the concept to the next level.
- Chapters 11 and 12 provide an overview of research approaches that can help you develop and evaluate your concepts. Chapter 11 focuses on qualitative

research to be used to both develop and refine concepts with individuals and small groups; chapter 12 focuses on better understanding how quantitative research works with testing your concepts with a broader audience.

- Chapter 13 focuses on potential differences among audience types and how these differences may affect the language and content of your positioning concept.
- Chapter 14 helps you understand how you can employ outside expertise to enhance your development and writing process.
- Chapter 15 helps you determine your direction after your concept is developed and qualified.

My goal in writing this book was to create a constant reference tool for you to use during any new concept-development project. The tips and techniques here have worked for my many clients over the years—and can work for you, too. Enjoy!

ACKNOWLEDGMENTS

I dedicate this book to my husband, John, who is my biggest cheerleader and best friend. Without his support and encouragement, I never would have completed this book. In addition to his own career, he served as the "mom" for our kids as I traveled for my various clients and wrote this book.

I also dedicate this book to my kids, Elise, Monique, and Elliot, who give me abundant joy and remind me not to take life too seriously. I have learned that hugs are always welcome, even when I'm sitting at my desk under a pile of work.

A special thank-you to my colleagues and friends, in particular Julie Kaufman and Sharon Walsh. Their invaluable feedback on my manuscript has ensured that this product is the best it can be. Thanks also to Linda Marholin of Quantum Insights, who provided her expertise in the quantitative research section.

Thank you to Procter & Gamble, which gave me my first job out of Harvard Business School. That is where all my concept learning started. The company helped me realize that one of the most enjoyable parts of marketing is understanding your target consumer and using that knowledge to create new concepts and effective advertising.

And finally, I thank all my clients whom I have worked with over the years. Each concept-development project has increased my knowledge of the subject—knowledge that can benefit past and future clients through this book.

CHAPTER 1

CONCEPT DEVELOPMENT

Apple iPod
Smart Car
Netflix
Ritz Carlton
Chanel
Disney...

Behind every successful product or service lies a powerful concept. It is really that simple. Product and service offerings that win in the marketplace are successful in presenting an idea that combines a clear benefit with invisible consumer logic. This combination produces winners, even in our noisy consumer environment.

According to various research studies, between 50 and 80 percent of new products launched each year fail,[1] costing companies and shareholders billions of dollars. This does not mean the only reason a product fails is the concept—the culprit could be lack of distribution, poor advertising, wrong media, and so on, but even if the concept were to blame in only a third of these failures, that still paints a pretty bleak picture.

One of the most notable product failures in history was New Coke, launched in the 1980s. Fundamentally, Coke missed the mark with this product because since 1969 the company had positioned the original Coke as "the real thing." People were unwilling to accept the new version because it was *not* "the real thing." After just ten weeks (and $4 million in market research), Coke reverted to what it did best: original Coke, which was now labeled "Coca-Cola Classic." Undoubtedly, the company spent a substantial amount of money on packaging, promotion, and advertising for New Coke, in addition to the initial market research.

The dictionary defines a concept as a general idea or something formed in the mind—a thought or a notion. Concepts come in many shapes and forms. There are advertising concepts, core-idea concepts, packaging concepts, and positioning concepts. My focus here is the very simple idea of a *positioning concept* for a product or service—also called a *marketing concept.*

For the purposes of this book, the term "product" will refer to services as well as physical products. For the most part they are interchangeable in terms of marketing; the

---

1   Charles Mayo and Deborah Hansler, "New Product Development," in *Reference For Business* (Advameg, Inc., http://www.referenceforbusiness.com/management/Mar-No/New-Product-Development.html (accessed January 15, 2011).

major differences between a product and a service are the aspects of a service that can be labeled "intangible." Service often comes in a variety of packages: lowest cost, highest quality, fastest, best value, friendliest, longest hours, and so on—all of which are less tangible than the qualities generally described in a product concept.

Every product in the marketplace combines two elements: the physical product that is being offered and the marketing—or positioning—concept that goes with it. So, what is a marketing concept? It is the mental picture of the benefit that consumers believe they will receive when they purchase a product.

Larry Huston of Procter & Gamble gave the best description of a marketing concept that I've ever heard:

> A true measure of a [positioning] concept is its simplicity. When presenting the concept to the consumer, [we] must provide a clean, easily defensible, clearly articulated, emotionally satisfying, thoroughly convincing, superior answer to the deceptively simple question, "Why should I purchase from you?"[2]

WHY SHOULD I PURCHASE YOUR OFFERING?

Your goal in concept development is to find an answer to this question and present it in a way that sparks your consumer's interest. Identifying a winning strategy for your product is critical, no matter the situation. Here are a few scenarios.

---

2   Larry A. Huston, "The Wealth Creation Power of a Concept" (speech, Cincinnati, OH., February 6, 1995.)

- *Your declining brand needs a new strategy.* This, of course, is the most obvious reason for developing a new concept. The first step is to make sure that the concept is indeed the problem. This means that you need to understand the drivers of your business with a thorough analysis *before* you start doing concept work. Could the decline be due to a lousy media plan, unrealistic pricing, lost distribution in a key account, or something else? Because any or all of those factors could impact your brand's performance, it's critical that you examine each one. Below I have outlined a variety of scenarios that might fall under the declining brand issue.

  - Your product enjoys high brand awareness but has lost relevance. Examples:

    - Polaroid Instant Camera (replaced by any digital camera)
    - IBM Selectric typewriter (replaced by personal computers)
    - Blockbuster Video (supplanted by Netflix)
    - Any delivered newspaper for folks under 50 (now online)

  - Your consumers are not loyal and select products by price only instead of seeing the benefits of your product. Examples:

    - Any product that loses substantial sales to a generic brand
    - Products replaced by a brand that stands for value (e.g. Suave hair products)
    - A first car for a new driver who just wants wheels!

- The brand strategy is no longer distinctive in the category and all the "me too's" claim the same benefits. Examples:

  - Pantene hair care successfully owned and show-cased a visual of healthy hair, which it communicated as "hair so healthy, it shines." Once competitors jumped in with the same claim, Pantene needed to adjust the concept to remain unique and relevant.
  - Hybrid cars have made the fuel-efficient small cars of the past look not so fuel-efficient.
  - Volvo, known for safety, has changed its strategy to "No one will be killed or injured in a new Volvo car by 2020."[3] More than likely, this stronger claim is the result of other car companies making similar safety claims; it is punctuated by independent rating agencies giving safety ratings for consumers to review.

- *You need products to fill unmet consumer needs.* Market conditions change over time. Something that was truly important in a category at one time may no longer be so. Think, for instance, about rising gas prices. For many years, Ford carved out a comfortable home with SUVs and large trucks. The company has had to rethink its product offerings, however, because the market is moving toward smaller, more fuel-efficient vehicles and hybrid technology. The day of the gas-guzzling "own-the-road" type of vehicle is starting to shift as gas prices remain high.

---

3   Ken Zino, "Volvo Cars Makes Bold Safety Claim: Zero" (*The Detroit Bureau*, September 25, 2009, http://www.thedetroitbureau.com/2009/09/volvo-cars-makes-bold-safety-claim-zero, accessed January 25, 2011.)

- *A new competitor has entered the market.* Frequently, a new competitor will come into the marketplace with a product that really shakes up the status quo. Consumers can be fickle; when they find a new product with some cachet, they are likely to switch loyalties. A great example is the Apple iPhone, which turned the cell phone industry on its head. The only way to get an iPhone was to have a contract with AT&T, and many people switched. To compete, many other cell phone companies started to imitate the iPhone. This provided the other carriers with products that plugged the holes in their consumer bases. In this case, concept development is really the only way to defend your product and maintain customers' loyalty. (In 2011, Verizon got operating rights for the iPhone, albeit with some limitations.)

- *You have new technology or service capability.* Often, something new comes along that you need to exploit. Although a new capability should typically be developed to fit a consumer need, sometimes product advancement finds an unexpected home. Rogaine is a great example: While scientists were exploring the treatment of hypertension (high blood pressure) with minoxidil (Rogaine's active ingredient), they discovered that one of the side effects was hair growth. Minoxidil was then tested for the potential to regrow hair for balding individuals. The results were impressive enough that the treatment was approved for people suffering from hair loss. A concept was created and successfully launched in the marketplace.

INVOLVING OTHERS

The heart of any concept-writing effort is your core team. While the marketing team often takes the lead, it's important to include individuals from research and development (R&D) and market research in the effort. Each department brings different strengths to the process. Marketing, of course, understands the business goals and the competitive landscape. It also has an intimate understanding of the needs and wants of the target audience. Even if the business type is new to an organization, such as through a recent acquisition, marketing will ultimately oversee the business portfolio. It will become knowledgeable in the aforementioned ideas as the concept-development research evolves.

R&D and market research act as the bookends to the marketer. Each one supports the marketer's efforts throughout the process in a unique way. Depending on the nature of the business, the R&D person serves as the knowledge source in a variety of areas. R&D knows what a new food will taste like, how a product works, or how a new service will be integrated into existing services. As a result, R&D can provide valuable insight into what areas can be claimed and supported in a concept. Market research is the voice of history and of the consumer. Often, the market research person will know what types of recent information are already available for the team to use in their effort. In addition, she serves as the person primarily responsible for setting up the research plan and ensuring that the team is getting feedback from the appropriate consumer(s).

You also should involve someone from your advertising agency. Generally, this role is best served by an account executive (or planner/strategist), *not* a copywriter. Many people are surprised when I suggest they disinvite the copywriter. The reason is simple: A concept is not advertising. A copywriter's talents are best used for the creative part of bringing a winning concept to life, not crafting the concept. Copywriters excel at crafting language that is clever, memorable, and catchy, but we don't need that skill to write a concept. However, involving an account executive, or the like, is perfect. He can serve as the liaison between the client, the brand team, and the creative team at the agency. In this role, he has a full understanding of both sides' needs and wants. He can also provide some objectivity to the process, since he doesn't live and breathe the brand or business every minute of his working life.

At some point, make sure you visit your legal counsel. The last thing you want is to develop an amazing concept that you can't support legally. Sometimes, crafty use of language can help to make a product claim legally defensible. The wording may be slightly different from the original proposed language, but the consumer takeaway is the same. This is not always the case, but it's certainly useful to know if it's not legally defensible before you get to the finish line. You don't want consumers to fall in love with something you can't say.

A CONCEPT COACH CAN HELP

Strong concept-writing skills are a rare commodity. This means that clients can often receive substantial value by involving a trained concept writer and coach who can bring much-needed expertise to the table. With my clients, I sometimes work simply as a coach and concept writer. At other times, I'm involved in the entire process, from ideation right through to consumer-qualified concept, refined in qualitative research. Engaging a coach can make a huge difference in time and money in the creation of a concept. Chapter 14 will describe this process in greater detail.

CONCEPT VS. COPY

Sometimes, concept development is not the right step for your brand or product. You may just need some strategic copy or advertising development to give your business a boost. Typically, copy/advertising development is necessary when you need to execute a sound business or brand strategy.

The copy-development checklist below can help answer your concerns. If you can answer yes to any of the scenarios, then copy development is a good next step. If so, pick up the phone and call your advertising agency!

Yes	No	
☐	☐	I have a winning concept that I need to communicate to my target audience.
☐	☐	I have new consumer insight that could freshen up my existing strategy.
☐	☐	I have a new way to communicate something about my product (a visual, a product demonstration, a new tagline, etc.).
☐	☐	I am broadening my current strategy to a new target audience, such as certain populations, or a new international market.

At this point, you should know whether concept development is what your business needs. So let's get started.

CHAPTER 2

SETTING THE STAGE

The first step of a successful concept-development initiative is to set the stage for the effort. Your goal is to create an initiative that is ownable, unique, desired, and relevant. Setting the stage sets you on the road to that goal.

Consider how much preliminary work goes into a theatrical performance. Among the many elements are a script for the play, actors for each role, a stage for the performance, and scenery to showcase the setting. The success of the final result—the live performance—depends upon the skill with which these and other components are executed.

Similarly, if you want your audience to love your new product, you need to set the stage for its concept development with care. Here are some things that you need to know before you start:

- What are the wants, desires, and needs of your target consumers?

- What emotions and feelings do your consumers hold about your product/category?
- What is your current brand equity (assuming your brand is established)?
- What does the current competitive landscape look like?
- What are the potential opportunities for the future?

Without this kind of information, there is a good chance that you will make a critical error at some point in your process. Just as a theatrical troupe needs to focus first on the script, the actors, the stage, and the scenery, you need to focus on your own preliminaries to ensure the successful "performance" of your product. Unfortunately, many concept-development teams tend to ignore these key preliminaries, preferring instead to dive in headfirst. This can be a costly dive.

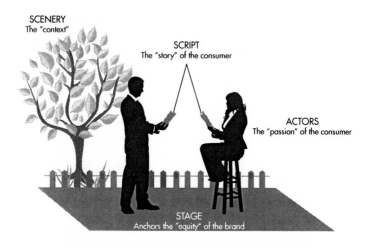

SCENERY
The "context"

SCRIPT
The "story" of the consumer

ACTORS
The "passion" of the consumer

STAGE
Anchors the "equity" of the brand

Let's look at the different steps that set the stage for a new concept-development initiative. The first step is the *script*.

SCRIPT: WHAT IS
YOUR CONSUMER'S STORY?

In the case of new concept development, the script needs to include the wants and needs of your target audience. What is their story? You want to understand not only their reactions to your currently available products, functions, and features, but also the reasons for their choices. A great first step is to thoroughly understand what benefits are being offered and if your customers are satisfied with them. Then you need to push deeper to identify areas of opportunity—that is, the ways in which your products are *not* providing your customers with the benefits they want. What issues do they have with your current offerings? How do they perceive the "ideal" or "perfect" solution to their needs?

There are many ways to discover more about your target consumers. The documents you need may already exist in your organization. While I do not advocate using reports from ten years ago, anything researched in the past three years probably has some relevance. I always encourage clients to do a little "history check" before jumping into a new effort. Sometimes, looking at information through a new pair of eyes or with a different goal in mind can unearth new insights. Why spend additional money and time on research if the organization already has the information?

If you discover useful existing information, then your team will need to sit down and review the material. To divvy up the work, I often recommend that small teams review different sections of the material and bring the key points to an information-sharing session. This allows the entire concept-development team to ground itself in the same information.

Once the team is well grounded, the information gaps will need to be identified and a research plan created to capture the additional information. In rare cases, all of the information needed to fill the gaps may be available within your company. Most of the time, however, the information regarding the habits, practices, and motivations of your consumers in the category of interest will need to be updated. This can be done qualitatively, using in-person focus groups or variations including mini-groups, quads, triads, dyads, and one-on-ones. If you desire a broader representation than a city or two, a qualitative online methodology might be more appropriate. Or, perhaps, when you need a more intimate understanding of a specific area, in-context research or some type of ethnography may be the right approach. Quantitative research can also have a place here, with surveys about satisfaction/dissatisfaction, habits and practices explorations, category understanding, or segmentation. Again, the strategic objective should always drive the research approach, instead of the other way around.

It is very important that you do not underestimate the knowledge available within your organization and from public sources. Internally, this source might be someone who used to work in the category or reviewed consumer complaints. External public sources of information can also be very useful. You might be surprised at what shows up when you conduct a public search, such as on Google, on a topic around your concept-development effort—or on a related subject. For example, if you are developing health and fitness products, you might gather useful information from a dietician's website. Not everything on the Internet is accurate, but reading through online information can raise pertinent questions or concerns. And, remember, your target consumer might be reading the same information on a website or in a social-media context.

At the end of the day, the more you understand about your consumer, the sharper your competitive edge will be. Your organization or brand will be more nimble as market changes occur—and this can make the difference between market leadership and declining share.

ACTORS: WHAT IS THE CONSUMER'S PASSION WITH YOUR PRODUCT?

Actors portray the emotions and feelings that bring a play's characters to life. Emotion, whether positive or negative, links the consumer to your brand, the category, or your specific product. This means that you need to assess consumers' level of engagement. When a tight emotional connection occurs, your brand often has more long-term traction. While features and promises can come and go, the emotion can stay with a consumer for a long time.

A product is more likely to break through the category clutter and be remembered when the target connects emotionally with it. When consumers are engaged, the offering becomes memorable. This engagement can create product differentiation that may not even be real. In this regard, I always think of the Hallmark card TV ads where some mushy backstory brings a lump to my throat. In the end, a Hallmark card is just a piece of paper with a message, but somehow I feel that spending the extra few bucks to "send the very best" seems worthwhile, in spite of numerous cheaper substitutes. Hallmark has successfully identified the hook that keeps me (and others) coming back.

If it turns out that consumers are not very engaged in the product or decisions around their choices, your concept-development effort may be much more challenging. Disability insurance might be good example. For many, incremental disability-insurance coverage involves choosing whether to check a box on one of many forms when starting with a new employer. In some cases, a young person might think that the odds are against needing extra insurance—and that is the end of that decision. Such a person probably would not want to listen to a pitch on disability insurance even if it provided very compelling information. This is a tough nut to crack; he may not change his mind until he or a family member has to step out of the workforce and sees the actual benefit of such a policy. By that time, it might be too late to make a purchase decision.

In contrast, a high-involvement category such as food engages virtually every consumer—especially it if involves chocolate or not having to cook a meal. In this case, identifying the functional need and any emotional benefits might be much easier for all involved. Think about McDonald's, which has many fast-food competitors. Its decision to advertise "healthy" sides to kids meals makes Mom feel better about going to McDonald's—even if her kids get the chicken nuggets and french fries.

Qualitative research is generally the best way to get inside a consumer's head to know how she thinks and feels. Whether in person or online, a researcher can explore these feelings deeply with techniques such as laddering—a qualitative approach where the participant identifies functional benefits and the moderator, step-by-step, "ladders" these ideas to higher-level emotional benefits. She might also employ a variety of projective exercises, such as collages, picture associations, verbal metaphors, or colors that project feelings, to get consumers to talk about their experiences beyond the functional needs the product meets.

SCENERY: IN WHAT CONTEXT ARE YOU DEVELOPING YOUR PRODUCT?

What is the scenery—the setting—for your performance? You must know the backdrop and context of the competitive environment to make informed choices before concept development. You need a clear understanding of the current marketplace, how the various competitors are positioned, and any barriers to entry. Your goal in concept development is to find "white space" in the market so you can own a distinct place in the consumer's mind.

Generally speaking, if a product doesn't have a clear position, then consumer perceptions will position it. A good example is the Pringles brand of snack crisps. Originally, consumers believed that Pringles was just another kind of chips that happened to be neatly stacked in a can so they didn't break. As it turns out, this belief did not embrace the full power of the product, which emerged when Procter & Gamble identified a positioning to communicate the uniqueness of the brand. Pringles was *not* a potato chip; it wasn't even greasy like a potato chip. Pringles was a fun, novel snack food. Most of us have been "popping the Pringles" (as early ads stated) ever since.

Both primary and secondary research can help answer context questions. For primary research, qualitative testing is a great place to start. Speak with current category users and learn how they perceive the market. You can accomplish this quite simply with sorting exercises or by using a tool such as a perceptual map to relate a competitive set and specific attributes on a two-by-two-inch grid (see the example below). In addition, you can identify usage habits and practices, as well as any market gaps.

Here's how a perceptual map for a variety of Honda automobiles might look when evaluated on fuel economy vs. price:

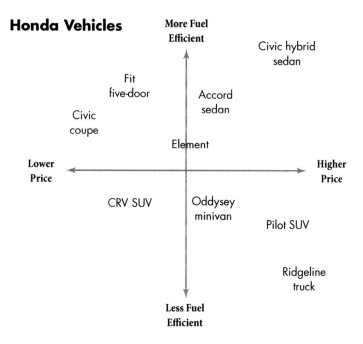

Honda Vehicles

From a secondary-research standpoint, try looking at the websites of competitors. You can gain a clear understanding of what they are telling their audience—how they see themselves as unique in the market. In addition, look at social-networking sites where a category's "users" can chat about issues and concerns. Finally, syndicated data may be found about a particular industry, category, or target demographic—for a fee.

STAGE: WHAT ANCHORS YOUR PRODUCT IN THE CONSUMER'S MIND?

The stage represents the brand equity or the heritage of the company. This anchors the performance and provides realistic guidelines as to how far the brand can be extended. Even if potential consumers do not use a product, they generally have a perception about it. In some cases, this perception might be the reason that they have not tried the product. Consumers might perceive it as too expensive, as could happen with a department store cosmetic, or as offering something they don't think they need, as might be the case with an organic or natural line of products. A product also could have an aesthetic some consumers don't like, such as a floral or fruit scent—or, perhaps, it requires too much use of technology. This exercise will help you understand barriers to trial—or windows of opportunity.

The stage might not be pertinent if you are establishing a new brand, but it is still important from a competitive standpoint. If you have a company that consumers associate with industrial chemicals, extending into upscale beauty products may be downright impossible. By contrast, a company known for bleach may have an easy time moving into other categories related to disinfecting, thanks to preconceived notions about the power of bleach.

Any successful positioning needs to reinforce the brand message. This helps the marketer create a story behind the business; that not only enhances any halo effect around existing offerings, but also saves marketing dollars.

THE PERFORMANCE

When all of these elements are carefully evaluated and you have all the information you need, you are ready to start the concept-writing process. To reiterate: Before embarking on any concept-development effort, you need to:

- thoroughly understand the wants and desires of your consumer—the "script."
- identify the current perceptions of the brand equity and/or company by your target audience—the "actors."
- know the competitive landscape—the "scenery."
- understand and be true to your brand equity—the "stage."

Just as in a theatrical performance, all these areas must come together and be well executed for the show to be a success.

CHAPTER 3

THE CONCEPT

A concept is fundamentally a representation of an idea for a product or service. With a definition that simple, it might seem surprising that so few professionals can write a great concept. However, the concept writer faces many challenges. I hope that by the time you finish this book, you'll feel comfortable and confident writing concepts that win in the marketplace.

Concepts come in a variety of shapes and forms. No one has really created an exact norm or standard for the ideal concept. Sometimes, concepts are a very simple framework with just a few phrases pulled together to create an image in the mind of the buyer. Some concepts consist primarily of pictures and graphics, while others are simply a whiteboard of text without a single picture. And many concepts contain both graphics and text.

Regardless of the form, any company that offers a product or service to some type of constituency needs to develop winning positioning concepts. For instance, a pharmaceutical company needs a compelling concept to persuade doctors to prescribe a medication. As the drug industry becomes more consumerist, with TV and print advertising, a compelling consumer concept also becomes necessary—and it is likely to be different and more basic than a concept that targets doctors. Similarly, two concepts may be necessary in a business-to-business environment, one for the procurement department and one for the ultimate user of the offering. And finally, a product or service needs a well-designed concept to articulate the unique place that it will inhabit in the life of the consumer. Remember, if you don't position your offering, the competition or the consumer will.

CORE IDEA VS. POSITIONING CONCEPTS

Two fundamental types of concepts exist: core idea concepts and positioning concepts. Most concepts comprise some elements of each. (More on that later!)

A core idea concept simply describes the product or service. For the most part, it is a relatively concise description of what is being offered to the end buyer. The purpose of a core idea concept is to determine whether the idea is of interest to the end buyer. Typically, a core idea concept does not attempt to sell any benefits to the potential buyer but will simply highlight some of the features the product or service offers.

> ## Core idea concept example for organic milk
>
> ### My Farm organic milk
>
> Introducing My Farm organic milk, with all the nutritional features of regular milk but all natural and free of artificial growth hormones. It is fortified with vitamins A and D and is available in 2 percent, 1 percent, and fat free. Find My Farm organic milk, in the dairy section of your local grocer.

In contrast, a positioning concept attempts to sell the benefits of the product or service to a potential buyer. The positioning concept must tap into real consumer beliefs that provide a relevant context for the product idea. A positioning concept focuses on the rational or emotional benefits a buyer will receive or feel by using the product.

> ## Positioning concept example for organic milk
>
> ### My Farm organic milk—the feel-good choice
>
> My kids are exposed to so much junk food and artificial ingredients in their food. I really want to help them be as healthy as possible.
>
> Now you can. Introducing My Farm organic milk—the milk you can feel good about serving. With all the nutritional features of regular milk, My Farm organic milk is all natural and free of artificial growth hormones.
>
> Available in the dairy section of your local grocer.

When comparing the two approaches here, you'll notice a few things about the positioning concept that differentiates it from the core idea concept:

- It has an emotional hook for differentiation.
- It has an insight that sets the tone for the target audience.
- It offers a specific benefit
- It is selective about its claims—it uses only the ones that truly support the benefit.

WHAT A CONCEPT ISN'T

Because there isn't one standard way to write a concept, the marketing world is full of different viewpoints on what a final concept should look like. Because of this lack of agreement, it's imperative to talk about what a concept is *not*.

Below I've created an example to show what a sample concept might look like for a made-up product called "Miracle Upholstery Cleaner." Although we'll get into more detail in later chapters, for our purposes here you should note that the first section speaks directly to the potential buyer as if she were thinking the thought to herself. The second section is what the company or brand is giving to the buyer, so it is written from the manufacturer's point of view. The final section provides the information that proves the manufacturer can deliver the promise made to the buyer in section two.

Now, let's use the "Miracle Upholstery Cleaner" to illustrate the various points about what your concept should not be.

Positioning concept

Miracle upholstery cleaner cleans and inhibits stain formation

It's hard for me to keep my furniture clean because my family spills a lot of stuff and my pets track in dirt. I vacuum the furniture, but I just can't seem to stay ahead of it.

Introducing new Miracle Upholstery Cleaner—it cleans your cloth furniture and helps prevent future stains.

Unlike other products, Miracle not only has proven surfactants for cleaning, but also contains a new ingredient, Impede X, that leaves an invisible protective coating on the cloth. Moisture beads up and dirt can't work its way into the fibers, which allows for easy cleanup any time.

Miracle Upholstery Cleaner—you'll rarely get a stain in the future.

A concept is not an ad. All too often, marketing clients turn to their advertising agency's copywriter to help with their concept-development efforts. The agency should be involved because ultimately it will need to develop compelling copy in some shape or form, and often an account executive or account planner can provide great strategic insight into the process. The intent of concept writing is to get the idea developed in a single-minded way that will be relevant to the buyer. In other words, "do they get it and do they want to buy it?"

However, this is not the time to add flowery language and plays on words, which is the specialty of the agency copywriter. Do yourself a favor and save those writing skills for creative development of copy or advertising *after* you've got the concept nailed down.

Too much like advertising

Miracle upholstery cleaner really is a miracle!

Just look at my furniture. I just can't keep it clean. My family and my pets—a spill, food, or dirt from the yard. Is there anything I can do?

Now there's Miracle Upholstery Cleaner. It cleans and prevents stains in your home like nothing you've ever tried before.

With Miracle, you simply spray to clean while leaving the rest of the magic to the product. Just watch as new Impede X penetrates the cloth while it cleans. The light foam shows it is working as it lays down a protective coating to prevent future stains. Miracle Upholstery Cleaner—in the household cleaning aisle.

Miracle Upholstery Cleaner—for unbelievable cleaning.

A concept is not a product label or an instruction manual. Sometimes, a business feels compelled to tell too much about a product. Perhaps it feels that it needs to let its audience know all of the details they would find on a product label. But as important as the label is, the purpose of concept writing is not to develop it. If you're working on a line extension, it may be important to give context to the mother brand, but that doesn't mean that every detail needs reciting. Instead, a "family" product shot might do the trick. Similarly, the end buyer should not expect to find every bit of information in the concept that she would find in the instruction manual.

It's important to closely scrutinize your concept and make sure that it doesn't get bogged down in unnecessary details. Listen to your consumers; if they don't "get it" because they are missing some critical information that completes the logic, then add that information. As a marketer, you need to decide what is critical to communicate to the consumer. If a product is relatively novel, then you may need to tell someone how to use it, but they don't need to know all of the instructions. It could be as simple as "Just mix a capful with a quart of water," or "Just one tablet every twenty-four hours." It doesn't need to include a full disclaimer or detailed instructions.

Too much like a product label

Miracle upholstery cleaner cleans and inhibits stain formation

It's hard for me to keep my furniture clean because my family spills a lot of stuff and my pets track in dirt. I vacuum the furniture, but I just can't stay ahead of it.

Introducing new Miracle Upholstery Cleaner. It cleans your cloth furniture and helps prevent future stains from developing.

Unlike other products, Miracle not only has proven surfactants for cleaning, but also contains a new ingredient, Impede X, that leaves an invisible protective coating on the cloth. To use, vacuum the furniture thoroughly, then spray on the cleaner. Let sit for five minutes, and when it starts to foam, you know it's working. It lifts the dirt up while leaving a protective coating on the fibers. Use at least every eight weeks to keep the furniture looking its best.

Miracle Upholstery Cleaner—you'll rarely get a stain in the future.

A concept is not an exhaustive list of every feature. Another term for this is the "kitchen sink" concept, a derivative of the phrase "everything but the kitchen sink," a phrase that implies the inclusion of almost everything, necessary or not. This is exactly what happens in the "kitchen sink" concept—a marketer feels that his product or service offers so many benefits and features that he must include them all for a winning concept. Because a "kitchen sink" concept has something for everyone, it often scores incredibly well in quantitative testing—but fails to deliver in the marketplace, because in the marketplace only one idea can be communicated in advertising and marketing materials.

An exhaustive list of every feature

Miracle upholstery cleaner cleans and inhibits stain formation

It's hard for me to keep my furniture clean because my family spills a lot of stuff and my pets track in dirt. I vacuum, but I just can't stay ahead of them.

Introducing new Miracle Upholstery Cleaner. It cleans your cloth furniture and helps prevent future stains from developing.

Unlike other products, Miracle not only has proven surfactants for cleaning, but also contains a new ingredient, Impede X, that leaves an invisible protective coating on the cloth. Impede X can be used on any type of fabric and won't damage the fibers or color. The product can last up to eight weeks without repeating the application and can be used more often if your furniture gets a lot of wear and tear. It is safe for children and pets. It comes both in a trigger bottle and aerosol for your convenience and is available in the household cleaning section of your favorite stores.

Miracle Upholstery Cleaner—you'll rarely get a stain in the future.

For you to develop a successful marketing strategy, the product needs to own a place in the market. Your core idea concept is simply not going to help you move to the next step. You need a positioning concept, so that's where we'll begin.

KEY THINGS TO REMEMBER:

✓ Know what type of concept you're creating. To market your product, you'll eventually need a positioning concept.

✓ Keep your concept simple and informative.

✓ Don't try to create advertising copy, a product label, or a laundry list of everything your product can offer.

CHAPTER 4

THE POSITIONING CONCEPT OUTLINE

Regardless of what form a concept takes during development, following some specific guidelines will help ensure that all of the critical elements are put in front of the consumer for feedback.

When you are in the process of building a concept, it will probably look different than the "final" concept that you place into some type of quantitative test. This is primarily because you don't need a lot of bells and whistles in the early-development phase. These elements, including versions, scents, and distribution channels, can add a lot of "noise" to the concept—and these distractions may hinder the developer in getting the blueprint right. These elements will be added later on to complete the story in concept testing.

In early development, it's essential to keep the concept very simple. It usually comprises just five basic elements:

- headline
- accepted consumer belief
- benefit
- reason to believe + any essential information
- wrap-up

In the initial phases of development, you can skip the headline and wrap-up until the foundational idea is solidified. But right now we'll take a look at all five elements.

HEADLINE

The headline captures the essence of the concept. It should include the name of the product and the primary benefit.

ACCEPTED CONSUMER BELIEF

The accepted consumer belief, or ACB, articulates the consumer insight that sets up the need for your product or service. Typically, it underscores the background and the problem that will make your offering the viable solution. It needs to demonstrate to the potential consumer that the company and the brand understand the consumer. Some companies call this the "statement of empathy." However, since a well-written ACB will naturally show empathy, this title can be superfluous.

In addition, sometimes clients will call this the "consumer insight." I believe, however, that there is a difference between an insight and an ACB. The consumer insight is the nugget or learning that reveals something about your target audience that you may or may not have known. By contrast, an ACB is the articulation of the insight, served up to the consumer in an acceptable manner. The examples below point to the difference between an insight and an ACB.

Consumer insight

Women over forty believe that women are perceived as old when they have gray hair and/or wrinkles, while men with the same characteristics are considered to have character and look distinguished.

ACB

I color my hair and care for my skin to help retain my youthful appearance. The last thing I want is to be seen as "old."

BENEFIT

The benefit is what the product will offer consumers to solve their unmet need or frustration. A benefit can be either functional or emotional.

REASON TO BELIEVE + ANY ESSENTIAL INFORMATION

The reason to believe, or RTB, provides the information the consumer needs to substantiate the stated product benefit. RTBs come in a variety of forms that we will discuss later; whatever form an RTB takes, however, it's critical that it make logical sense to the consumer.

In some situations, the concept may need additional essential information to hold together for the reader. For example, if a concept for an air freshener is being developed, it will probably be essential to let the consumer know that is it available in a specific number of scents. However, in the early part of the development process, listing all scents and forms would not be essential to understanding whether the entire concept holds together.

WRAP-UP

The wrap-up simply brings closure to the concept by restating the primary benefit in a slightly different manner.

Example of a basic concept

Here is an example based on this very book.

HEADLINE	WRITE SMARTER CONCEPTS WITH "MARKETING CONCEPTS THAT WIN!"
ACB	Writing a positioning concept can be very challenging for a variety of reasons. I wish I could know what the experts know when it comes to developing concepts.
Benefit	Introducing "Marketing Concepts That Win!"— the new resource book that focuses on helping you write better positioning concepts.
RTB + any essential information	The book is filled with essential background information as well as many tips and tricks that the author has employed successfully with real clients. The result has been the creation of winning concepts for their offerings. You can read the entire book—or just the parts that focus on your problem areas.
Wrap-up	"Marketing Concepts That Win!"—knowledge for you, winning concepts for your product.

WHITEBOARDS

In the early rounds of development, a concept typically is shown on a simple whiteboard or a whiteboard with a picture. The term "whiteboard" simply means the concept can be typed up on the computer, printed on a white piece of paper, and distributed to a respondent for feedback. In the past, these printouts were often mounted on foam board so they could be held in front of a group. Clearly, the concept can be on any color of paper and doesn't even need to be mounted on a board. But the basic idea of the whiteboard is to communicate a concept in a manner that the respondent can easily understand. A whiteboard concept for this book would look similar to the example on the previous page, only without the different elements listed in the left column.

A whiteboard might be embellished with an image or illustration that captures the most important aspect of the concept. In some cases, this might be a functional representation of what the product offers; in other cases it might capture the emotion that the concept is trying to express. In this particular example, a picture is probably not critical because the idea is simple and an image of a book cover wouldn't enhance understanding. However, if the concept happened to be Apple's MacBook Air computer, a visual probably would be essential to communicate the idea. Such a visual would clearly help respondents believe that the product was the thinnest computer available.

In a final concept, a visual is generally a good idea, and a standard procedure to help solidify the concept communication. Unfortunately, often the concept and its associated visual evolve on different time frames, so that when the "final" concept is pulled together, a mismatch can

Example of a whiteboard concept where an image might be critical

New Apple MacBook Air,
ultrathin and ultraportable

Photo used with permission from Apple, Inc.
Photographer: Andrew Bettles

I carry my laptop with me all the time because it's critical to my productivity. Unfortunately, once I include all the cords and batteries, it adds a lot of weight and bulk to my briefcase.

Introducing the new Apple MacBook Air, the laptop that is ultrathin and ultraportable.

Apple rethought convention in creating the thinnest laptop available in the market. Encased in less than an inch of sleek, sturdy anodized aluminum, it weighs just three pounds.

Apple MacBook Air, the world's thinnest notebook computer.

occur. The solution is to make sure that the picture represents some form of consumer reality. You don't want to set up false expectations of the product experience—such as the wrong package size or a rendering that doesn't even remotely match the actual product. It is imperative to check how consumers perceive the "fit" of the picture with the written concept.

During the past 20 years, we have come to expect ever more rapid flows of information. Recipients of information are required to process and respond more quickly than ever before. We expect instant information with plenty of visuals and text, whether the medium is a text message, Twitter, CNN Headline News, or a music video. A picture may prove critical to connecting with a particular potential audience. You do not want the consumer to create his own image of what you're trying to convey—so, where possible, add a visual or video.

Whether you select a picture early or late in the development process, make sure that it undergoes consumer review to determine the fit *before* a quantitative test. These research studies are expensive, and you really don't want an inappropriate picture to detract from the concept, especially if your idea and positioning are sound. A mistake like that could easily impact your test results, which, in turn, might alter your purchase intent—the "go/no go" decision.

IDEAL CONCEPT—FORMAT AND LAYOUT

Once you know that you've got the right idea captured in a single-minded concept, the finalized concept may include some or all of the elements listed below:

- brand name
- price
- size(s)
- versions
- product illustration or image
- trade distribution channel
- if it's a line extension, reference to the baseline

A positioning concept format you could use is shown below. It is not critical to follow this layout precisely, but the areas listed above, which truly affect purchase intent, should be outlined. In addition, if you are testing concepts against each other either qualitatively or quantitatively, you don't want to allow the format to skew the acceptance. As a moderator, there is nothing worse than hearing, "I like this one better because the format is better."

Brand- and benefit-focused headline

Picture or illustration

[ACB in consumer language.] [Issue or frustration your product will solve.]

Introducing Product ABC, the [product/service category] that [benefit with action verb].

That's because Product ABC [reason to believe support points pertinent to benefit].

Product ABC—[wrap-up with benefit stated in different words].

Product ABC comes in [size] and costs [amount]. Find it [where].

4KidsOnly Cell Phone—
one less stressor for a parent

Photo used with permission from istock.com.

Determining the right age for a child to get a cell phone is tough. I want to know I can reach her or she can reach me when needed, but I don't want the phone to become a distraction at school or during other activities.

Introducing the 4KidsOnly cell phone, the phone that gives parents peace of mind.

That's because the 4KidsOnly cell phone has the functions of a regular phone, but also allows the parent to pick the desired available features, such as a limited address book and control options for texting, games, the Internet, and more.

The 4KidsOnly cell phone—rest assured that your child is a phone call away.

Available for just $49.99 anywhere cell phones are sold. In six fun colors. Can be added to your existing cell phone plan with any carrier.

To review, a concept comprises five basic elements:

- headline
- accepted consumer belief (ACB)
- benefit
- reason to believe (RTB) + any essential information
- wrap-up

When you are in the initial stages of building a concept, you need to focus on capturing the essence of the concept. You should leave off the various bells and whistles—they will be included later on. You can even omit the headline and the wrap-up and just concentrate on the ACB, the benefit, and the RTB.

These initial stages are a good time to decide if your concept needs an illustration to communicate the most important aspects of the concept. If you do choose to include an illustration, you will need to run it through a consumer review to determine if the picture "fits" the words in the concept.

KEY THINGS TO REMEMBER:

- ✓ All positioning concepts need, at minimum, an accepted consumer belief (ACB), a benefit, and a reason to believe (RTB).
- ✓ In early development, use an image only if it helps communicate a potentially confusing idea.
- ✓ In a final concept, make sure your target audience has reviewed the image and that it fits with the concept. You don't want the wrong picture to turn consumers away from a great idea.

CHAPTER 5

"CLeAR" THINKING FOR BEST CONCEPT WRITING

An effective positioning concept is not just about writing words for your idea that you think your target consumer would like to hear. It is really about finding the sweet spot at the intersection of three critical areas: *c*ontent, *l*anguage, and *r*elevance—or "CLeAR."

Let's explore each area so that we can fully understand the importance of each to the final outcome.

CONTENT

Content includes both the basic concept elements and the "story" around the idea. The basic elements of the concept must be present from the beginning. In early rounds, this

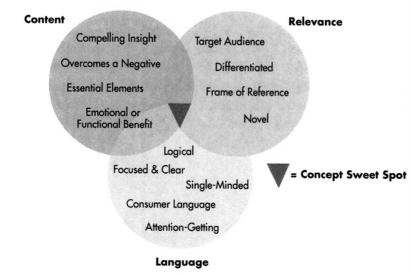

would include the accepted consumer belief (ACB), the benefit, and the reason to believe (RTB). Additional factors such as size and pricing can be added in later rounds. While these pieces are the starting point for a complete concept, you will need to make certain choices to ensure that you craft the best concept. Here are some key questions that you should ask:

- Does the overall concept overcome a current negative or solve a problem in the marketplace? Is the issue real?
- Does the concept offer a functional benefit or an emotional benefit?
- Is the ACB compelling? Does it set up the need for the benefit?
- Is the RTB strong and believable?

Overcome a negative or meet an unmet need

Probably the most important aspect of content is whether it is meaningful to the potential target audience. I don't care how fantastic your product or service is—if it doesn't provide the consumer with a real solution to some challenge, it probably won't have much traction in the marketplace.

In some cases a product or service may address a need that the consumer really did not know he had. Smartphones are great examples. Although technology was moving in the direction of a portable communication device and an office in our hand, did anyone really think that applications could be created for just about anything? Many of us never imagined that we might photograph a bar code to discover the best price for a product in our area. Did you guess that you could track calories, find out when weather has closed your child's school, or get instant notification of flight changes while in transit? But now, many of us can't imagine life without these devices!

Benefits

Generally, concept development involves coming up with a variety of concepts for testing purposes. As such, you're likely to have some concepts with functional benefits and others with emotional benefits. You might even have some of both. So what's the difference?

A functional benefit focuses on the more *tangible* claims that a product or service can provide. Often these benefits focus on the most prominent aspects of the offering.

Examples of functional benefits include a cell phone company with the largest network, a fertilizer that expedites seed maturation, and a bank with the best mortgage rates in the area.

An emotional benefit focuses on the *feelings* around the experience of interfacing with the product or service. Because these benefits seem much more subjective, they need to be carefully worded to maintain credibility.

Examples of emotional benefits include: the brand of car you'll be proud to call your own, the insurance product that makes you feel in charge of your health, and the product that convinces you that you've made the right choice.

Regardless of the type of benefit, the content must be supportable from a legal standpoint. Corporate advertising lawyers ensure exactly that (I was lucky—I married one!). So don't let your creativity run away with you; some quick checks with your product-development folks and your lawyers are definitely in order. The last thing you want to do is make claims that can't be substantiated.

Accepted consumer beliefs (ACBs)

A compelling ACB needs to "speak" to the target audience. We'll talk more about capturing the communication appropriately in chapter 9, but from a content standpoint, an ACB has to be based on a compelling insight. All too often, I've seen clients who just make up some kind of insight that has nothing to do with their target consumer; it just "sounds good." In order to create a winning concept, you have to do your homework and thoroughly understand your consumer. Otherwise, you won't know what problem or frustration you're trying to solve with your offering. This means that the ACB should set up the benefit naturally; if it doesn't, you've got the wrong ACB.

Reason to believe (RTB)

The RTB completes the logic of the concept. The consumer must understand how this product or service is going to improve her life. It must add credibility to the product promise—hence the term "reason to believe." The RTB outlines the relevant support points that make the concept airtight. It's not a laundry list of everything you can offer; only the salient points should be included. Anything else merely adds confusion.

LANGUAGE

Language is all about how you communicate the concept to your target audience. Probably the most important aspect of this communication is the use of *consumer language*—putting the concept in the consumer's voice. Everyday people don't talk like manufacturers. I'm amazed at the number of concepts I see to which the end buyer can't relate. You need to speak to your audience in the way they speak. Think of it like a parent: Would you really speak to a two-year-old the same way you'd speak to a teenager? Of course not (and, fortunately, the two-year-old doesn't want the car keys). Your language needs to relate to the person you're speaking to—not to the management of the company behind the product.

Here are a few examples of the kind of ACB manufacturer-speak I've seen:

Manufacturer-speak 1

So much has changed in the past twenty years; we now have microwaves, computers, and cable TV. So it is crazy to imagine that you're managing your household finances the same old way.

In this particular example, it sounds like the manufacturer is talking down to the consumer. The takeaway seems to be, "You're crazy . . . " This is clearly not a way to draw the consumer to the product and entice his interest.

Revised using consumer language

So much has changed in the past 20 years that makes our lives easier—like computers and cell phones. I'm not sure why I am managing my finances the same old way.

Manufacturer-speak 2

You're the head of your home and make all the important decisions. What about disability insurance? This is a very important decision you make for your family, but you're probably thinking, "It won't happen to me."

Such a message could make the target audience feel pretty stupid. At minimum, it seems to aggressively put thoughts in the consumer's head.

Revised using consumer language

I haven't thought that much about disability insurance. I just figure that it won't happen to me, so I haven't bothered with the additional cost.

In addition to employing consumer language, your concept presentation needs to be absolutely clear—so that the consumer knows what you're talking about. If your target audience has no idea what you're trying to communicate, then they won't understand your offering. A good part of this clarity requires keeping the language uncomplicated—making it something a fourth grader can read. Remember, a typical commercial is only thirty seconds long; you can't communicate a complicated idea in that period of time.

I've seen two-page, single-spaced concepts that are about as clear as mud. For brevity, here's an example of an RTB for a basic cleaning implement that is not only complicated but also somewhat off topic.

Complicated

> One side is extra thick and bumpy while the other side is smooth and soft—so it's kind of like the two-sided brush you use to clean and polish your shoes. The bumpy side is designed for cleaning and scrubbing, but flip it over and the smooth side adds that polished or finished touch to any of a variety of cleaning jobs.

Try to communicate that in thirty seconds!

Clearer

> One side is designed for cleaning and scrubbing, but flip it over and the smooth side adds that polished or finished touch to any job.

Single-minded

Keeping a concept single-minded is also important. What benefit do you want to focus on? Since marketers often can't decide, they instead may load up one concept with a lot of benefits. Of course, you can argue that these multifaceted benefits will have at least one aspect that will appeal to everyone. But when this concept is to be turned into advertising, where is the focus? It's pretty difficult to turn any of these ideas into a good copy (or communications) strategy when the concept developers can't focus on a single, clear benefit.

Here are a couple of examples of concepts that include too many benefits.

Too many benefits

Introducing a new frozen-meal line that is healthy, great tasting, and easy to prepare.

Three claims: health, flavor, and prep.

Too many benefits

It's finally here: a fuel-efficient sports car that is fast, sleekly styled, and affordable.

Four claims: fuel economy, speed, styling, and cost.

Getting attention

Finally, you want the concept to be attention getting. This does *not* mean it is advertising. I'll say that again—it is not advertising. Getting attention is about projecting energy and excitement—finding a hook that excites or intrigues a prospective consumer. It is not about having cute slogans and a great jingle. That comes *after* the concept.

To get the right kind of attention, the tone of the language needs to be positive even if you're solving a negative issue.

Negative attention

I dread tax time. Getting all of my papers together, filling out forms, writing checks, meeting deadlines—I just don't want to do it.

This might get attention, but it will be negative attention.

Better

Tax time isn't my favorite time of the year. I'd really love a way to make the whole process easier.

Of course, you have to be realistic. No one can get totally excited about taxes!

RELEVANCE

Last but not least, your concept must be relevant to your target audience and perceived as novel and unique in the competitive landscape. Relevance to your audience links directly back to language and content. You have to know not only whom you are talking to but also how they think or speak about the issue your product or service is trying to overcome. Even a desirable offering will come to nothing if it is not served up in a way that is meaningful and relevant to your consumer.

Of course, you need to bring something novel to your competitive set—something that differentiates it from similar offerings. Sometimes, simply being first is the key to success. Think about the Amazon Kindle. While electronic readers were slow to gain acceptance, once Kindle created and "owned" the marketplace, others joined in. But those entering needed to provide something new and different to lure first-time buyers. This manifested in such areas as color screens and the ability to download books from multiple sources. If the products were just like a Kindle, then folks would likely just buy a Kindle.

Finally, the concept must provide a meaningful frame of reference, or context. This allows the target audience to see how the offering fits into their world better than any competitor. Apple's series of Mac vs. PC advertisements is a good example of high-impact messages that provided context. This ad campaign showcased montages of challenges a personal-computer user might experience. *Adweek*, a weekly advertising trade publication, named it the best ad campaign of the decade in late 2009. PC manufacturers punched back at Apple with the "I'm a PC" campaign, which was all about the qualities of the individuals using the computer, rather than the functionality of the machine.

PLANNING AND POLITICS

Concept development can be a fun and exciting process. However, depending on the nature of the product or service and how much business revenue it is expected to create, it can also be a political nightmare. Different levels of management desire different levels of involvement. For example, sometimes the chief marketing officer is an integral part of the development and signs off at each key milestone, while at other times the oversight is provided by a group of individuals.

The key to dealing with company politics is careful planning and alignment early in the process. A core team of concept developers needs to be identified and fully committed to the project from the start. Generally, this does not mean that research findings are reported to them for their stamp of approval. Instead, it means that these individuals are in the trenches and working together on every step. Let's call this the "core team."

The core team is responsible for creating the overall objectives and clearly explaining how this effort fits into the overall business goals. Whether this is done in an informal statement or a formal written document, it's critical that the team know who in management needs to sign off at each key milestone.

While the core team should embrace management feedback when appropriate throughout the process, they should not fall into the trap of having management rewrite every concept for them. That is impractical and fraught with difficulties because the members of management making suggestions have not been a part of the entire process. They often do not have the information necessary to support their suggestions and may derail the concept-creation process.

If senior management does need to sign off and embrace changes but is not part of the core team, you will need to allow plenty of time for this signoff. I know, I know—these are the people who "need it tomorrow." But I've seen too many concept-writing efforts that were dead in the water after many thousands of dollars were spent in research efforts. So give yourself the luxury of plenty of time to report findings with each block of learning so the core team *and* management can move in the same direction.

Here's an example from a client of the challenges involved in working with management.

I worked extensively with a team developing concepts based on foundational research through an iterative process. After working for three days, we ended up with several unique approaches, each of which was worthy of moving forward into a quantitative test. When the "final" concepts were returned to senior management, they offered their improvements. Unfortunately, this review completely changed the key driver of one of the concepts, which happened to leverage the idea of empowering the user.

While writing the report after qualitative research, one of the key areas I mentioned was how the women really grabbed onto the idea of feeling empowered. Fortunately, the idea was brought back into the concept by the same management who had nixed it in the first round. In the quantitative test, the "empowered" concept emerged the winner when shown on its own or with a forced choice, driven primarily by the "feeling of empowerment" the women felt.

Remember, your consumer is the one who buys your product or service—so tell her what she wants to hear. And make sure your management hears it, too!

ART OR SCIENCE?

Concept writing is both art and science. I wouldn't have written this book if I didn't feel that writing a concept requires some science. There are guidelines for structure and many rules of thumb to follow—rules I learned from one of the best concept-development companies in the world, Procter & Gamble. Since that time, I've learned by doing and created many tips and tricks for improving your concept writing. That said, writing a *simple* concept is not easy—just ask any of my clients. Most people struggle to communicate simple ideas with just a few words (a struggle that might date to the days when the "heaviest" paper got the best grade in ninth-grade English class). The art comes when you can communicate the core idea in your concept in fewer than a hundred words!

KEY THINGS TO REMEMBER:

- ✓ Remember to be "CLeAR" when crafting your concepts—a good concept exists at the intersection of content, language, and relevance.
- ✓ Make sure you understand the organizational sensitivities and the politics around your concept-development effort.
- ✓ If you understand the science of writing a concept, the art will come with more experience or with the help of a trained expert.

CHAPTER 6

BENEFIT

Now we are finally ready to start writing concepts. Basically, I view the writing of a concept as a run around a track. Like any race, you have a starting gate, laps to complete, and a sprint to the finish.

START WITH THE BENEFIT

So we are now at the starting gate. You always want to start with the benefit statement because if your consumer isn't interested in what you have to offer, nothing else is going to make much of a difference. The purpose of the benefit statement is twofold: First, it illuminates the accepted consumer belief (ACB) around a frustration or unmet need; second, it describes the main advantage that the product or service offers to the target audience consumer. Simply stated, a benefit promises a compelling answer to this question:

What's in it for me?

Two basic types of benefit statements can be developed for most ideas: functional and emotional. We touched briefly on these in chapter 5.

Functional/product benefits relate directly to what the product or service can offer in *objective* terms to the end consumer. Functional benefits describe the performance that the consumer gets from using the product. Examples might include a wireless phone company advertising fewer dropped calls or a bug spray advertising that it kills insects.

Emotional/human benefits relate directly to what the product or service can offer to the end consumer in *subjective* terms. Emotional benefits describe the personal value that the consumer gets from experiencing the product. Here are some selling lines that were driven by an emotional benefit.

> "When you care enough to send the very best."
> —Hallmark cards
> "Every kiss begins with Kay Jewelers."
> "Have a Coke and a smile."

Emotional benefits can often be much more difficult than functional benefits to craft and get consumer buy-in for. Nevertheless, they can add a level of distinctiveness that often provides a competitive advantage in the marketplace. In addition, emotional benefits can often add more drama and interest to advertising than functional benefits. Both types are worth pursuing when you develop concepts.

The four E's of benefits

When developing consumer-driven benefit ideas with clients in ideation sessions, it is generally easiest to divide claims into four categories. This will ensure that you and your team don't miss any areas that should be mined. These "benefit buckets" include:

- **equity**—derived from the heritage benefit of the brand
- **efficacy**—grounded in formula- or service-based claims
- **experience**—based on appealing to the senses of sight, smell, and touch
- **emotion**—based on personal feelings about the process or final outcome

To bring these four E's to life, let's look at a hypothetical example of a new line extension for a brand called Miracle, which we used back in chapter 3. Although the new line will focus on cleaning furniture upholstery, the brand has a heritage in laundry as the toughest in-laundry stain remover. So let's look at all the different kinds of benefits that could evolve from this product and its heritage.

Equity-based:

New Miracle Upholstery Cleaner removes tough stains that others leave behind.

New Miracle Upholstery Cleaner removes tough stains without scrubbing.

Efficacy-based:

New Miracle Upholstery Cleaner cleans and prevents new spills from becoming stains.

New Miracle Upholstery Cleaner delivers professional cleaning results.

Experience-based:

New Miracle Upholstery Cleaner—for noticeably cleaner furniture.

New Miracle Upholstery Cleaner cleans and brightens the entire room.

Emotion-based:

New Miracle Upholstery Cleaner helps you feel confident that your home is clean and healthy.

New Miracle Upholstery Cleaner makes you feel like your furniture is brand-new.

While efficacy claims are based on the product and emotional claims are based on feelings, the equity- and experience-based claims are not so clear-cut. The nature of the offering and the company's history of interaction with the end consumer will generally drive these claims.

As an example, think about the Woolite brand in relation to washing delicate clothes and a potential claim for a line extension.

Experience-based:

New Woolite now safely cleans your dark-colored delicates.

Equity-based:

The trusted cleaning of Woolite, now for dark clothes.

Often, as consumers, we find ourselves surprised at how something we perceive as very functional can actually be laddered to a very emotional place.

For instance, thanks to the cotton growers, we've been introduced to the idea that cotton is "the fabric of our lives."

Thanks to Folgers coffee, we know that Folgers is "the best part of wakin' up."

Over years of helping clients write concepts, I have learned some helpful tips to maximize the benefit-development exercise. I find that using "before" and "after" examples tends to make all of this come to life in a more compelling manner.

Make it distinctive for the category

Whatever category you're working in, it is imperative that the benefit be distinctive and ownable. If everyone else in the category can make same claim, it isn't going to create any traction in the marketplace.

BEFORE—not ownable

Brand Q hair color removes the gray.

Okay, let's get real. If you are over thirty and the hair color doesn't remove the gray, you aren't even going to consider buying Brand Q! Of course, if I were a teenager desiring a green streak in my hair, I wouldn't buy it either, but that's not the point because teens are clearly not the target audience.

AFTER—more distinct

Brand Q hair color gives six weeks of nonstop color.

Now I get it! The marketer has come up with a claim that could create some traction. Basically, this new benefit also implies that the gray has been removed but elevates the promise to a much more distinctive and ownable platform. And frankly, as someone over 30, removing the gray is just expected!

Use "you"—the second-person singular— in a benefit

When you are writing a benefit statement, using the second person can help aim a benefit at your target audience. Consider the following examples:

- Now Amazon offers you free delivery for orders over $50.
- Introducing improved Luvs diapers that give your baby heavy-duty protection.
- With Geico insurance, you'll save more money vs. the other leading insurance companies.

While this sounds very basic, it is important to know that in the benefit portion of the concept, the manufacturer or service provider is giving something to the consumer. A benefit almost always has a verb because the company is providing some product or service to make the consumer's life better in some way. In other words, the company needs to emphasize that it is giving or providing you with something.

A slight exception is called for when your concept is focused on an intermediary distributor, as in the case of marketing a consumer-advertised prescription drug to doctors. In cases like these, the "you" would be tweaked to focus on "your end customer." For example: "Introducing prescription X, to give your patients relief from heartburn." Or, for carpet distributors: "Now you can supply the full-weave, luxurious carpet that your client stores will love."

Stay single-minded so your consumer "gets it"

This is probably the biggest challenge that most marketers face. They want to claim everything they possibly can to try to sell the product.

Before—too complicated

Brand Z hand lotion minimizes age spots, reduces lines, and leaves your hands soft and smooth.

This very complicated benefit would be extremely difficult to execute in the marketplace because so many different ideas are being presented. It would be impossible to determine which area should be the primary focus in advertising.

After—simplified

Brand Z hand lotion gives you younger-looking hands.

Now we've elevated the functional laundry list of benefits to a higher emotional plane. I think most of us would agree that "younger-looking" encapsulates the big idea for the consumer—and that her expectations are probably that it does all the things listed in the "before" statement. Not only have we simplified the communication, but we've also revised the concept to a more emotionally charged promise of looking younger.

In some cases you may need to include what I call the "cost-of-entry claim" in order to take your consumer to the higher-order benefit. This doesn't violate the single-minded rule because your concept is not going to focus on that claim; instead, it provides assurance that the consumer will receive the basic expected benefit.

Include a "cost-of-entry" benefit (if a category requires it), plus something

A cost-of-entry benefit is basically a required benefit that must be included to be a competitor in a particular category. In some cases, it might be obvious, such as with a shampoo—it is expected to clean hair. Including such a benefit may seem obvious, but marketers often omit it, at the expense of negative consumer feedback. Save yourself the aggravation and just include it at the start, if the product or service isn't self-explanatory.

Here's a great example of how this kind of omission might occur: Consumer testing regarding a liquid for carpet-cleaning machines supported the insight that when a dirty carpet is cleaned, the entire room looks more brilliant and alive. Armed with this information, the marketing team excitedly created this benefit idea—and it got completely trashed by respondents in qualitative testing.

Before—missing required benefit

> Brand R for rug steam machines makes your whole room look brighter.

What was the problem? Just this: The process of steam cleaning a carpet is very onerous. It's necessary to move all the furniture out of the room, stay off the carpet while it dries, and then move the furniture back in. Consumers needed to be reassured that if they were going to make the effort to do all of this, the carpet would indeed be well cleaned—that they weren't just getting brighteners dumped on the carpet.

After—included required benefit

Brand R for rug steam machines deep cleans your carpet and makes your whole room look brighter.

A simple but necessary addition to the basic product promise took the benefit idea from loser to winner. It's hard to believe that five words—"deep cleans your carpet and"—can make such a difference, but clearly they can.

Make sure your concept is important to the target consumer

As I've mentioned previously, any concept-development effort needs to flow from consumer understanding and knowledge. Even when an idea flows from this learning, the articulation still might not fly when shown to consumers. This is where qualitative research can be so helpful. You must get feedback to get it right. Research, research, research!

Another area that is particularly challenging in categories with very functional benefits is claiming superiority. For the most part, you want to leverage any area that can differentiate your offering. If possible, offer superiority to other products in the category.

Here are three examples of claimed superiority:

- Brand K facial-care treatment clears up your skin better than other leading brands.
- Brand S sunscreen provides unmatched UV protection.
- Pepsi tastes better than Coke.

If you can't claim superiority, then you might consider power-parity claims. A power-parity claim makes it sound like the product or service offers something superior. In reality, the consumer simply infers superiority for an offering that is essentially equal to its competitors.

Power-parity claims

No face-care treatment clears up your skin better than Brand K.

No face-care treatment beats Brand K at clearing up skin.

Before you go any further with statements like these, you need to be certain that they are legally supportable—so double-check with both your research and development and legal departments.

Fit with brand character

Finally, it is critical always to remember who you are and where you live in the consumer's mind.

As I mentioned in chapter 5, any new concept must fit within the framework of the brand if the promise is to be believable and ownable. If it doesn't fit, the potential consumer confusion may completely negate anything new you're bringing to your constituency.

Here are some imaginary examples of products that don't fit the framework of their brand:

- The Woolite brand (stands for gentle, caring, effective, delicates) developing a tire cleaner for cars.
- Raid insect spray (stands for tough and effective) developing a facial moisturizer.

- Ben & Jerry's ice cream (stands for fun, innovative, premium taste with lots of cream) making a full line of diet products.

In contrast, a brand such as Tylenol, which stands for safe, gentle, and easy on the stomach, might create products for infants and children. Because the core adult brand identity is already well established, these new products would fit nicely with the established brand equity.

Now you need to challenge yourself to add discipline to your benefit writing. It's time to get your team together and give it your best shot.

KEY THINGS TO REMEMBER:

✓ Develop both functional and emotional benefits for your product or service offering.

✓ In your development efforts, remember the four E's: equity, efficacy, experience, and emotion.

✓ Start with the benefit and get it right before you develop the rest of the concept.

CHAPTER 7

ACCEPTED CONSUMER BELIEF

Hopefully, you now know which benefits resonate with your target audience, and you can start building your accepted consumer beliefs (ACBs) for your concept. Crafting an ACB is often the hardest part of the process because you need to set up the context in a way that is meaningful and relevant to your target consumer. In terms of a time frame, I view this step as "rounding the bend" on a racetrack because you may need to rework it several times before you get the language just right.

The ACB communicates the unmet need or frustration that your target consumer feels. It provides a fundamental context for the entire concept. Get it wrong and the concept becomes confusing and irrelevant. Get it right and the concept will flow forward effortlessly. Of course, this forward flow also assumes that your benefit and reason to believe

(RTB) provide the solution and information required to fulfill the consumer's needs and complete the logic in a believable manner.

ACBs can come in a variety of formats, but they must somehow demonstrate a fundamental understanding of the needs of the consumer. Here are some typical approaches.

- Set up a consumer problem or conundrum:

    - "I worry about the long-term effects of taking a drug daily."

    - "I want to stay home to raise my children, but we can't afford it financially."

    - "I understand the need for disability insurance, but I'm young and it seems likes a waste of money."

- Communicate a frustrating current belief or notion:

    - "I want my delicates to get clean in the washer, but I don't want to ruin the fine fabrics."

    - "I love ice cream, but it is so fattening."

    - "Polished nails look so professional, but when they chip I look unkempt."

- Create a context for competitive positioning:

    - "Most hair conditioners make my fine hair flat."

    - "Soap leaves my skin feeling dry and tight."

    - "I don't feel as safe in a small car."

....

TIP 1:
Use consumer insight to craft your accepted consumer beliefs

....

As obvious as this sounds, you'd be surprised at how often clients start making up ACBs that have nothing to do with what the consumer says.

Now, you may be wondering if there really is a difference between a consumer insight and an ACB. I'd argue again that there is. As I mentioned earlier, insight is the learning, emotion, and experience you gain from your target audience, while an ACB is the *articulation* of that insight in a format that makes that target consumer nod her head and say, "Yes."

....

TIP 2:
Great ACBs follow "FOCUS IT"

....

You need to keep seven primary areas in mind when writing strong ACBs. You can easily remember these using the acronym "FOCUS IT."

F: Favorable tone
O: Once
C: Conversational
U: Unadorned
S: Statement

I: "I"—first person
T: Terse

I'll elaborate on each area so you can see how each of these can impact your communications.

Favorable tone

The nature of an ACB makes a favorable tone particularly challenging, because when you set up a problem to solve, people aren't usually smiling and happy about the situation. This is a place where the choice of words and the tone of the communication can make a huge difference. Here's an example that might help bring it to life for you: an ACB that could be related to some type of grocery-store discount card that saves shoppers money.

Before—negative

Gas and food prices are so high, I'm finding it difficult make ends meet. I am not sure how I am going to keep food on the table. I just don't see any hope that prices will get better soon.

This statement is very negative and exudes hopelessness for the consumer. You can't expect to win over a consumer with a great new idea if you've dragged her down into depression. Choosing lighter language and articulating optimism about saving money, on the other hand, would be welcome. Consider the example below.

After—more positive

The high price of gas and rising food cost has gotten everyone talking. Anything to save a few bucks is welcome.

Softening a negative statement

Occasionally, using qualifying words that help lighten the communication and make it less absolute can soften a negative statement. Definitive statements that sound negative and commanding can make consumers shudder.

Examples of common qualifying words are

- Sometimes
- often
- occasionally
- periodically

Such words can give people a polite "out." Read these before and after examples aloud and you'll hear the difference.

Before

After a long day at work, I just don't want to cook dinner for my husband and kids.

After—softened

After a long day at work, sometimes I just don't want to cook dinner for my husband and kids.

The change is minute, but adding that one word gives a consumer the permission to say, "Yeah, that happens once in a while," instead of being offended that the brand or company is implying that the mom is always too lazy to cook for her family. If you think I'm splitting hairs, take heed of the difference when a concept goes into a quantitative concept test. Often one of the key criteria to move forward based on the test is likelihood of purchase or purchase intent based on what is explained in the concept. If the key success percentage of purchase intent is 40 percent and your concept scores 39 percent in the test, you'd probably rather make this tweak to maximize your possibility of success. Minor adjustments can often sway a consumer in your favor.

Once

Restating the benefit is a natural tendency when we write concepts, but resist it and give the information one time only. Repetition happens primarily when a writer tries so hard to set up the benefit that he says the same thing twice. When I'm working with clients in person, we call this the "barking dog." Yes, it is a funny name, but take a look at the example below. Incidentally, this name provides a great mechanism for feedback from team members when we write concepts together. Anyone in the room has permission to "bark" or "woof" when she hears a concept presented that restates the benefit. Trust me, it always happens!

ACB + benefit

I really enjoy animals. I've always wanted a dog that barks.

Now, introducing the barking dog.

The "barking dog" ACB can take a variety of forms, but generally you will see things framed in the manner of a wish or a want. As a reminder, the ACB is written in the first person and the benefit in the second person because the manufacturer is offering something to you, the reader of the concept.

ACB + benefit

My feet ache after a long day of standing at work. I wish I could get some comfort during the day.

Introducing Dr. Z's inner shoe soles, for all-day comfort for your feet.

ACB + benefit

Sometimes I just forget to take my daily medicine for condition X. What I really want is medicine I can take once a month and otherwise forget about.

Now you can, with Brand ABC, the first monthly medicine for your condition X.

Conversational language

Regardless of who your target consumer is, you want to use their language. If you are talking to doctors, you will need to use the language that is appropriate to them—even though this may be markedly different than the language you would direct to consumers. If you are talking to IT folks, then computer lingo may be appropriate. If you talk to everyday consumers about a benefit, be sure to speak their language, too. This is an area where smart qualitative research can really help out. Qualitative research can inform you about the words people use to describe a challenge and can help you avoid "manufacturer-speak"—which is, sadly, all too common in concepts.

Before—manufacturer-speak

It's thirty minutes 'til kickoff time, and you have a house full of hungry guys. That's when you realize you don't have enough food or snacks! Or maybe you're having a family gathering and six extra people arrive. In situations like these, a time-crunched mother can feel stuck.

This is overhyped. First, the ACB sounds like some kind of windup toy. It reads like we are cranking up mom to self-destruct. I almost get breathless as I try to read this idea aloud. Try it—you'll see how crazy it sounds.

In addition, everyday people just don't talk this way. I know, because I am a mom who often feels time pressure. But I'd never refer to myself as a "time-crunched mother," even if the sentiment were true. This designation sounds more like a marketing department's psychographic label for a specific market-segmentation study than a consumer's self-perception. Somehow, I can't imagine any mom introducing herself with "Hi, I'm a time-crunched mother. How are you?"

After—conversational language

Getting together with my friends and family to watch a game or hang out is fun and relaxing. But there's nothing worse than realizing I don't have enough food for everyone.

The tone of the entire ACB is much more comfortable and relatable once the language is cranked down a notch.

Use the "Starbucks Test" for consumer language. The Starbucks Test is really simple: If you wouldn't say something to your friend over a cup of coffee at Starbucks (or another favorite coffee shop), you haven't captured consumer language.

Unadorned

When you write ACBs, you should subscribe to the idea of "less is more." It's important to communicate what you need to say, but it's just as important to be economical with your words. When an ACB includes too much information, it often encourages the reader to dismiss particular elements and respond with, "That doesn't really refer to me."

Clearly, that is not what you are trying to accomplish. You want consumers to agree with the issue value of the concept and move on to find out more information, ultimately leading them to make the purchase.

Unfortunately, I've worked with many clients and consultants who believed that packing the concept with many ideas and insights was a winning strategy. It may improve concept scores because it is a "kitchen sink" concept, but it will be nearly impossible to isolate the specific drivers of interest when it comes to developing advertising copy.

Before—too complicated

At the end of a long day, there's nothing more relaxing than kicking back in the comfort of your living room, ordering takeout, calling up your friends, and putting on a hot new movie release. Unfortunately, the video store never seems to have the movies you want to watch.

Now, with Movies-on-Demand, you can watch what you want, when you want to see it.

When you tell a consumer their behavior, they may reject it. The prescribed behavior may not fit their particular situation. For example, the complicated ACB above may solicit feedback like:

- "I don't order takeout—it is too unhealthy."
- "I prefer to watch movies by myself."
- "I don't have any friends."
- "I watch TV in my family room, not my living room."

To many consumers, this ACB simply won't ring true.

After—unadorned and simplified

I love watching a movie at the end of a long day to relax, but the video store can be a hassle.

Now, with Movies-on-Demand, you can watch what you want, when you want to see it.

In this example, the "after" concept communicates the same idea but has broader appeal. The ACB lets the reader fill in the blanks instead of prescribing them for her.

Statement, not a question

It is very important that you write a declarative sentence rather than pose a question. For whatever reasons, marketers and R&Ders think that asking a question helps to engage their consumer. But, generally, questions put you in the world of copy/advertising instead of the world of concept creation. You can use a question in copy once you've fully developed the idea and clearly understand the target audience.

In a concept, however, a question is a high-risk proposition. The last thing you want to do when you set up your concept with the ACB is give the consumer the opportunity to answer "No." If anyone answers the question that way, then there is no basis for your product or service. Over and out—they are out of the concept and you don't have a new buyer. Consider the examples below.

Before

Sporting events are lots of fun. Are you looking to take your family to a premiere sporting event?

Possible answers to this question:

- "Yes, I'd love to do that."
- "No, I hate sports."
- "No, I don't think sporting events are fun."
- "No, premiere events are too expensive to be a family activity."

It just isn't worth the risk that you'll get any version of "no" for an answer. Below, I've eliminated the question and tweaked the statement to set up a problem.

After

Sporting events can be lots of fun, but premiere sporting events are too expensive for me to take the whole family.

The consumer might say, "No, the events aren't too expensive." That is great learning! Now you know that you have the ACB wrong—not that you asked the wrong question. You can fix it and move on.

"I"—the first-person singular

Your goal is to make a personal connection with the reader of the concept and to show empathy for the situation. Using the first person in the ACB helps to create that interpersonal context. When you use the second person (you) in the ACB, you'll hear feedback along the lines of "How do you know how I feel?" Or "I don't want you telling me what I think!" A simple switch from "you" to "I" can make a world of difference.

You might recall from chapter 6 that the benefit should be written in the second person. In that circumstance, the manufacturer or service provider is giving the buyer something. Using "you" to tell consumers that the brand gives them something makes sense. The benefit is not as personalized.

Read these ACBs aloud and hear the difference in tone just by switching the pronouns.

Before—second person

Your family loves your dog and you can't imagine what you'd do if he ever got lost.

After—first person

My family really loves our dog, and I can't imagine what we'd do if he ever got lost.

The only exception is when you are dealing with some type of intermediary. For instance, a concept focused on a doctor prescribing a medicine to a patient might suggest "your patient" in the third person, based on the nature of the relationship of the product to the ultimate end user.

Terse

It is critically important to focus on just one area of insight at a time, keeping it terse and single-minded. If you load up the ACB with multiple problems it becomes unbelievable that the product or service you're offering could resolve so many issues. In addition, when the concept is turned into copy, the advertising agency won't know which element of the ACB really drove the concept logic.

Before—multiple issues

Coloring my hair can be such a chore. Sometimes I get the wrong color, it stains my skin, and it can be so difficult to apply and use, too.

Basically, three problems are outlined. It's always better to break them into individual concept ideas to test which area is truly the biggest concern and how your offering can alleviate the issue.

After—ACB 1

Coloring my hair can be such a chore. It is hard to know if I've selected the correct color.

Try XYZ, for the hair color you want, every time.

After—ACB 2

Coloring my hair can be such a chore. I don't like how the color stains my skin.

Try XYZ hair color plus wipes for easy cleanup.

After—ACB 3

Coloring my hair can be such a chore. The color can be so difficult to apply and use.

Try XYZ hair-color applicator. It colors without the mess.

As you can see, teasing the ACB apart into three unique ideas could lead to three somewhat different concepts.

You should now be ready to start writing those ACBs that will spark the interest of your consumers.

KEY THINGS TO REMEMBER:

✓ Use consumer insight to craft your ACB.
✓ Great ACBs follow "FOCUS IT."

CHAPTER 8

REASON TO BELIEVE (RTB)

The reason to believe, or RTB, is the part of the concept that lends credibility to the product promise made to the consumer. It is critical to the concept because it explains to the user exactly why the product or service will deliver the benefit. Fundamentally, the RTB must complete the consumer logic, or the concept won't hold together.

For most teams, the RTB is the most difficult part of the concept to write, primarily because it requires integrating the function of the product or service with a thorough understanding of how the end consumer thinks about the offering. Just throwing a bunch of facts or statistics at a consumer doesn't ensure that the RTB will be meaningful. Often, the simplicity with which a consumer reviews an idea is vastly different from the professionals' view of what the product or service can offer.

Four basic types of RTBs can be developed for most concepts. A concept team should consider developing RTBs from all four approaches, even if it believes that some approaches won't work. This is not a waste of time; just the exercise may showcase something new and different that the team needs to think about.

LOGICAL APPROACH

This is the simplest of all RTBs. Basically, the logical approach simply explains how the offering solves a consumer problem. For the most part, the consumer will nod his head in agreement as he sees the "fit" of this RTB with the rest of the concept.

Let's look at the success of Halls cough drops. Although the Hall brothers started their business in 1893, the brand broke through the clutter in 1930 with the creation of the Mentho-Lyptus formula. This combination of menthol and eucalyptus in the drops provided the famous "Vapor Action" that has been pivotal to the brand's success.

Why was the Vapor Action the key? Because in those days, steam from vaporizers was the only way to relieve sinus and chest congestion. These fantastic little drops had something in them that acted just like the steam that consumers had already been using. So the logical explanation that supported the benefit of cough relief was a drop with vapor action. This fit with both the consumer belief about relief and the product's deliverable. To this day, Halls is a leading brand for solutions to cold and sore-throat symptoms.

A logical approach like this will generally work very well if it is easy to understand and conforms with consumer beliefs about how things are supposed to work.

Here's another example.

Benefit

The bleach tab that allows you to bleach without the mess.

RTB

Each tab contains the cleaning power of half a cup of bleach compacted in an easy-to-use tab. Simply drop the tab in your wash along with your regular detergent and you're done.

Often, this type of RTB can have even more impact if the product offers a tangible attribute or package that further supports the benefit. Following up on the bleach mess issue:

Product-attribute RTB

A tablet form can't spill like liquid bleach.

Package-related RTB

The package has a built-in dispenser that releases just one tablet into each load.

HISTORICAL BRAND EQUITY

When a consumer has had a satisfying relationship with a product or service in the past, the historical brand equity can leverage the acceptance of a new offering from the same manufacturer quite effectively. This acceptance results from the positive equity associated with that brand.

As easy as this sounds, few brands are able to sustain themselves on positive equity alone. In some cases, just the mention of the brand in a concept creates positive feelings or even opens receptivity to the offering. In most cases, however, the RTB would not rely only on the equity but would marry the name to the brand to help carry the offering. As an example, consider Olay facial-care products. For years, Olay has stood for facial care, particularly moisturizing. Linking Olay to "Regenerist" in a product line suggests that these anti-aging products will help regenerate the skin.

For a historical equity–type of RTB to be effective, a few critical success factors must also be in place.

First, the brand has to have a reputable track record, established over a period of years. It is highly unlikely that the "new kid on the block" will enjoy such a position. Examples of brands that have been able to successfully leverage their history include Smucker's, Coca-Cola, and Volvo. By contrast, a brand such as Woolite, known and trusted for delicate washables, had a difficult time moving into other areas such as dry-cleaning kits and rug cleaners. Its equity essentially acted as an anchor, impairing the brand's extension into new areas, even though those areas were related to its historical equity. That anchor, however, has been successful in allowing Woolite to own fine washables.

Examples of successful brand equity

Smucker's—"With a name like Smucker's, it has to be good."

Tide—laundry cleaning excellence

Apple—hip, cool, easy-to-use, innovative approaches to technology

Second, the brand needs to enjoy high brand awareness among its current and potential buyers. Without strong awareness, all the benefits in the world will not create acceptance. Think of Lysol, a brand that stands for highly effective germ killing. Not every Lysol product may have enjoyed overwhelming success, but any concept that includes the Lysol name likely will benefit from a halo effect of consumer awareness. This awareness has allowed the brand to successfully expand from a simple aerosol product into an entire array of widely accepted kitchen and bath cleaning products.

Finally, the new product or service needs to be highly consistent with what the brand has offered in the past. Let's consider Apple, which has had great success in reinventing itself. Even though Apple already had a stronghold in the market for school computers, the success of innovations such as the iPod, complemented by highly effective PC-bashing advertising, seeded the market for widespread acceptance of other products. These products, including the iPhone and the iPad, focus on no-hassle usage and novel applications of technology—key brand equities for Apple.

OUTSIDE ENDORSEMENT

An endorsement from a prominent outsider can be extremely compelling in adding credibility to an offering. These outsiders may come in the form of a well-known professional or professional organization, a research study from an independent party, a celebrity endorsement, or a patent. Here are some notable examples from the past and present.

Endorsement from a well-known professional person or organization

Restasis—for tear production, recommended by an eye doctor (Dr. Alison Tendler)

CPR certification—endorsed by the American Heart Association

The success of an outside endorsement depends on two factors: First, the source must be viewed as a true authority in the subject area, and, second, the source must be neutral—that is, not driven by special interests.

Celebrity endorsement

Weight Watchers—Sarah Ferguson, Jennifer Hudson

Nike—a variety of professional athletes

The primary challenge of a celebrity endorsement is that it generally requires some type of ongoing investment on the part of the brand. A celebrity or organization will want some remuneration in exchange for its endorsement.

You may have noticed that, for a while, Pepsi was loading up advertisements with the likes of celebrities such as Beyoncé. Although this was clearly an image-related approach, Pepsi has since pulled back. This may be due to extraordinarily high costs and/or the fact that most people don't relate to the lifestyles of the rich and famous. In addition, it probably didn't help that some of their "top dogs" have come in and out of favor, most notably Michael Jackson and Britney Spears. Similarly, we all witnessed the fall from favor of American golfing legend Tiger Woods, who was a spokesman for Pepsi's Gatorade brand. Clearly, such falls are a risk with any celebrity.

Research study

Trident—"four out of five dentists recommend sugarless gum for their patients who chew gum"

Tylenol—"the pain reliever hospitals use most"

At some point, a research study must be conducted to continue to support the claim. If the claim no longer holds, you may be out of luck or challenged by a competitor. Claim support is not a place to cut corners. As you probably know, the legal standard set by the Food and Drug Administration is that every advertiser must be able to substantiate that *any* claim is "truthful and not misleading." While there are many (many) nuances around the question of to whom "truthful and not misleading" applies, I would encourage you to engage the able services of a professional advertising lawyer when crafting a support plan, and then evaluating whether the results of any claim-support testing meet the required legal threshold.

Patent

Any drug that can't be produced in a generic form

Roundup—Monsanto built a huge herbicide business with patented glyphosate starting in the 1970s (the patent expired in 2000)

In its initial life, a patent generally suggests that nothing like this product is available on the market. Over time, consumers' impression that a patented product is unique changes, given that the patent eventually expires and generic forms become available.

FACTUAL EVIDENCE

Typically, factual evidence can be incredibly compelling, though often difficult to explain with words alone. For this type of RTB to succeed, the product must be shown in action so that the consumer can experience the benefit. We've all seen this kind of action in commercials with side-by-side comparisons or with before/after demonstrations. These are usually seen in products with strong efficacy benefits. Examples might include seeing spotless glasses coming out of the dishwasher after using Cascade, a side-by-side torture test on a stained shirt treated with Spray 'n Wash, or a Volvo automobile after a crash test.

The challenge for the team in the concept developing and writing phase is to create a demo that shows the product actually working. This does require some preplanning to "test" these ideas with consumers as development proceeds. In most cases, showing an extreme "torture test" for the product is desirable from a consumer standpoint. But this means that the product must really deliver without raising concerns about it being too harsh or unsafe.

In addition, the result must be something that the consumer desires. While someone might really desire spotless glasses from their dishwasher, he might not really care if a new steak knife can cut through a leather shoe. Most of us don't cut too many shoes, and a visualization that suggests the knife never dulls might raise the fear that it's actually dangerous—that it might cut off your finger.

Tips and tricks

....

TIP 1:
Avoid techno-speak

....

Given that we have a diverse team working on a concept-development project, often the team knows *too much* about the product or service. As a result, team members may feel compelled to share everything they know to demonstrate the superiority of their product. This will typically result in "techno-speak"—that is, information that the consumer really doesn't care about.

While some might argue that the statement below teaches consumers something they didn't know, those consumers might ask if they really want a product with peptides and lycopenes in their hair.

Unnecessary techno-speak

At last, there's Brand X, a new hair-care line for fine hair that really delivers volume.

Unlike other hair-care products, Brand X contains amino acids to penetrate and strengthen hair, plus a combination of volumizing peptides and lycopenes for extra lift.

The stated RTB may create some questions and concerns about these various ingredients. Although the product contains these ingredients, the consumer probably doesn't see the logic due to a lack of familiarity with them. As a result, this RTB will probably provide confusion rather than clarity.

In contrast, the approach Pantene hair care employed when the brand was successfully restaged in the 1980s was an RTB that made a lot of sense to the average consumer. Most people knew that taking a vitamin orally would provide health benefits. So extending the idea of a "pro-vitamin" worked very effectively without a lot of unnecessary explaining.

A hair-care product with straightforward consumer logic

Introducing Pantene hair care, "for hair so healthy, it shines."

That's because Pantene contains a pro-vitamin B-5 complex that penetrates into your hair to help prevent damage from the inside out.

. . . .

TIP 2:
Keep the benefits in the benefit statement— don't squeeze them into the RTB

. . . .

Remember that at the end of the development process, your concept needs to be turned into copy or another type of marketing communication (see chapter 15). This basically means that a copy strategy needs to be developed with the goal of supporting just one outstanding benefit. One of the biggest challenges for marketers is to avoid the temptation to slip in a bunch of additional benefits just in case something can better explain what they are trying to communicate. The problem then becomes which benefit to focus on in the copy.

Too many "additional" benefits

New Brand X "One-Step" paint enables one-coat coverage.

That's because "One-Step" paint combines the primer and the final coat all in one paint, so it eliminates all the extra steps and work required with a typical paint job. You can complete the job faster, often in less than half the time, while making your walls look beautiful.

This concept has invited a variety of different benefits into the RTB. If the core team really believes that all of these areas are worth mining, they should be developed as independent concepts to truly test the value of the proposition. Here are several ways that this concept could be served up to make it more single-minded:

Benefit 1

New Brand X "One-Step" paint enables one-coat coverage.

Benefit 2

Introducing new Brand X "One-Step" paint—to complete your paint job faster.

Benefit 3

Introducing new Brand X "One-Step" paint, which eliminates priming your walls before you paint.

Benefit 4

New Brand X "One-Step" paint helps create beautiful walls with less work.

Exploring each of the ideas on their own merit will help the team develop a more executable marketing concept.

....

TIP 3:
Make sure the RTB supports the benefit with some inherent logic

....

The RTB needs to flow naturally while supporting the benefit. When this doesn't happen, the concept often becomes multifaceted. This can leave the consumer desiring to know more about exactly how the product or service successfully delivers the benefit—and maybe wanting to know more about the new information presented in the RTB.

Before—nonsense logic

Oven cleaners are effective, but they smell nasty and make me choke when I try to use them.

Introducing the new Brand P oven spray scrub sponge, which cleans without the smell because it contains a patented ingredient that dissolves burned-on food.

In the example above, an issue of no longer choking on fumes is raised, but it doesn't get satisfactorily answered in the RTB. Instead, the RTB has added a new dimension about dissolving food, which by itself might be quite interesting. The consumer would probably want to know more about dissolving the burned-on food.

Improved—more intuitive logic

Oven cleaners are effective, but they smell nasty and make me choke when I try to use them.

> Introducing the new Brand P oven scrub sponge, which cleans without the smell because the cleaning agents are embedded in a disposable sponge. Simply wet, wipe, and throw away.

The revised version, unlike the first one, has a relatively tidy response about the benefit of less smell while cleaning. The consumer can easily understand that a sponge with the product embedded requires no spraying, and thus no fumes that make you choke. This simple concept has completed a logical story that flows easily and is probably believable. Whether this motivates a purchase is a different story, but at least the consumer is not left feeling unsatisfied or confused by the explanation.

Overall, you must think carefully about which type of RTB will not only support your claimed benefit but also provide the most traction with your consumer. In some cases, the RTB claims may already have been proven; at other times, you may find that the most desirable RTB may need additional testing to ensure legal support.

KEY THINGS TO REMEMBER:

✓ Avoid confusing your consumers with techno-speak in the RTB.

✓ Keep the benefits in the benefit statement, not the RTB.

✓ Make sure that the RTB is logical; avoid confusing statements.

CHAPTER 9

THE FINISH LINE: PULLING IT ALL TOGETHER

At this point, you should have the three key areas of your concept fully developed: the accepted consumer belief (ACB), the benefit, and the reason to believe (RTB). Now, we just need to add the finishing touches—the headline, the summary, and any other essentials that must be communicated.

THE HEADLINE

The purpose of the headline is to summarize the most important idea. If we refer back to the purpose of a concept, it is to answer the consumer's question "Why should I purchase your offering?" To do that, the headline should focus on the benefit to the consumer; otherwise, we will have missed the point.

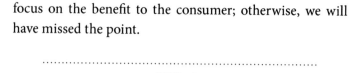

TIP 1:
Focus on the primary benefit

While you don't want the headline to say exactly what you've said in the benefit, you must remember to keep it fairly close. Simply find a slightly different way to say what the benefit states. In the example below, the headline is almost an exact copy of the benefit line. Therefore, it's not as impactful as a statement that implies the same idea but uses different language.

Before—too close to the wording of the actual benefit

EverHeat ski boot insoles keep feet warmer

I love to ski in winter, but my feet get so cold that I can't stay out on the slopes for more than a few runs.

Introducing the new EverHeat ski boot insoles, which keep your feet warmer than any ordinary thermal socks.

The insole features a specially designed inner core that creates heat when compressed by the foot in the ski boot. It also contains a proprietary insulation that maintains the heat inside the boot for up to three hours.

**Improved headline—states the benefit
in slightly different language**

EverHeat insoles: Keep your feet
comfortably toasty while skiing

I love to ski in winter, but my feet get so cold that I can't
stay out on the slopes for more than a few runs.

Introducing the new EverHeat ski boot insoles, which
keep your feet warmer than any ordinary thermal
socks.

The insole features a specially designed inner core
that creates heat when compressed by the foot in the
ski boot. It also contains a proprietary insulation that
maintains the heat inside the boot for up to three hours.

Here we've introduced the idea of "comfortably toasty,"
which suggests that your feet will stay warm while skiing.
The benefit punctuates the communication by suggesting an
"er" comparative claim (warm*er*), adding a competitive bite.

TIP 2:
Write the headline last

Building off our last point, since the headline summarizes
the concept, it should be written last, after you've fleshed
out the ACB, benefit, and RTB.

As obvious as this sounds, many clients tend to write concepts sequentially: headline, ACB, benefit, RTB, and summary. This really doesn't make sense, because the headline is supposed to encapsulate the concept. Back in my days at Procter & Gamble, we wrote what was called a "promise board" as we created our concepts—and I often do this with my clients (see the example on the facing page). This is particularly helpful because it allows you to review the key elements of the concept more objectively. It is based on the same principle as proofing a written document by reading right to left instead of left to right. Reversing the order helps you focus on the individual elements (the words); it doesn't allow your mind to fill in the blanks with what you meant to write but might have skipped.

As you can see, the numbers on the left refer to the final order of the elements, but here these elements are listed in the order in which a concept should be developed. As we mentioned above, you'll notice that the headline is *last* in the promise board.

Once you reorder the promise board, you've got your concept framework with preliminary thinking already outlined:

1. Headline
2. ACB
3. Benefit
4. RTB

The promise board also helps the core team determine if it is too hung up on certain elements of its concept. Generally, this happens in the RTB because everyone loves to relate all of the great things about their product or service, whether these things actually support the benefit or not.

Promise Boards
For a Single-Minded Proposition

3
I promise you or I promise you will: _____

_____

_____

_____
            Benefit

2
I know that is important to you because:_____

_____

_____

_____
            Insight/Accepted Consumer Benefit

4
You can believe and trust my promise because:_____

_____

_____

_____
            Support/RTB

1
To summarize, I promise: _____

_____

_____
            Headline

TIP 3:
Don't add new benefits to the headline

As you've read, each concept should be single-minded. Just be careful when you write the headline that you don't add new, unrelated benefits into the offering. I've seen concepts with three benefits—one in the headline, one in the benefit line, and another one in the summary line. Remember that this concept, if it is a winner, ultimately needs to be turned into advertising communication in one form or another. You simply can't have three benefits in successful copy.

Example headline—adds new benefits not related to primary benefit

EverHeat Skin Boot insoles—the fashionable and economical way to have warm feet

I love to ski in winter, but my feet get so cold that I can't stay out on the slopes for more than a few runs.

Introducing the new EverHeat ski boot insoles, which keep your feet warmer than regular socks.

The insole features a specially designed inner core that creates heat when compressed by the foot in the ski boot. It also contains a propriety insulation that maintains the heat inside the boot for up to three hours.

In this headline, we've added some new ideas that stray too far from the main benefit we're trying to communicate. In the copy, we haven't suggested any reason why these new insoles would be either fashionable or economical. These statements take the concept in a different direction; they are not aligned with the current RTB.

Another helpful way to think about the headline is that it must be able to stand alone; it must contain everything that the reader needs to remember about the primary essence of the idea. That means the headline should have the product name *and* the primary benefit. Think about it. In the end, you want your target to think, "I need that item." To accomplish this goal, you need to make it easy for her to remember the brand and the primary benefit.

....

TIP 4:
Treat the headline as if it is all the consumer will remember

....

I am sure you've watched a few commercials that struck you as funny or clever, but later you couldn't remember what was being advertised. This has happened to me during several Super Bowls. In cases like these, some companies will blow most of their media budget for just one thirty-second spot. Even though they are broadcasting to a huge audience, when a spot doesn't seed the mind with the brand, it's not going to generate the desired effect. Given this phenomenon, make sure your headline is not flat or boring. Here's an example for a toothbrush:

Boring headline: A new type of toothbrush

More engaging headline: With the SpinClean toothbrush, you get cleaner teeth in less time

Since the headline is written last, it should naturally bubble up to the top based on all the other work you've already successfully done. The easiest way to accomplish this is by using this formula:

Brand Name + verb + primary benefit (using language not in the concept)

While the headline does not have to be in this exact order, these primary elements should always be included. Here are several variations on the SpinClean toothbrush from the earlier example:

> Have cleaner teeth in less time with
> the SpinClean toothbrush

> With SpinClean, get the clean
> teeth you want faster

> SpinClean—get cleaner teeth, in less time

....

TIP 5:
A headline is not a print ad—it need not be provocative or attention getting
....

Finally, let's remember the purpose of the concept. The concept is not an ad, so the headline should not try to be some type of catchy selling line or slogan. Doing it this way might create the same situation as the Super Bowl ads where provocative headlines are remembered simply for being provocative, not for linking the unique selling proposition to the brand name.

Below are two examples of headlines that sound too much like advertising.

> EverHeat insoles—the coolest way
> to stay warm while skiing

> EverHeat insoles—warmer feet, hot skiing

THE WRAP-UP OR SUMMARY LINE

Like the headline, the wrap-up is simply a short recap or summary of the primary concept benefit. It reminds the consumer how the product or service will make his life better in some way if he uses the offering. It serves to "wrap up" the concept with a neat little bow for the consumer.

TIP 6:
Use different words for the wrap-up than for the benefit, but imply the same thing

Benefit: New XYZ breath mints leave your mouth tingling with freshness.

Wrap-up: Try XYZ breath mints to refresh your breath.

OTHER ESSENTIALS

The nature of the concept and the category norms will determine what other elements are essential for the concept to be complete.

Product positioning concept

Typically, a core idea concept needs to identify the sizes available, the price, and any variations in a line or family of products, such as versions or scents. These elements will often serve as reassurances that your product falls within the category norms and will answer certain concerns the consumer may have about your product. For example, people who are allergic to nuts might need an assurance that a food is made in a nut-free environment. People with sensitive skin might need to know that products are hypoallergenic or available in unscented versions.

When developing concepts, I usually suggest that these elements be minimized, unless they are essential for believability. They can add a lot of "noise" to the effort and get in the way of garnering feedback on the core idea. These elements can be added toward the end of the feedback cycle, but not until you know that you have the foundational elements nailed down. Normally, the critical elements will come up as questions from your consumer in qualitative research (for instance, "Does this come in unscented?").

TIP 7:
Core idea first, other essential information later

Examples of other essential pieces of information:

- Available in 2 percent, 1 percent, and skim in the dairy section of your local grocer
- Available in six delicious flavors in the snack aisle
- Floral, Fruit, and Unscented varieties
- Six-ounce cream, ten-ounce lotion

Service positioning concept

A service concept may also have some essentials, but it differs from a product concept. Typically, a service may need to provide information about how to set up an appointment or arrange for a visit. Alternately, it may need to provide information on insurance or a service guarantee.

Examples

Call 1-800-123-4567 or you can book online at www.service.com for a consultation.

First Union Bank is FDIC-insured.

Available only for first-time customers.

CLASSIC PITFALLS

Up to now, we've concentrated mostly on how to do things right. But it's also worth highlighting some of the classic pitfalls in concept writing. Learning about these kinds of disasters should help you to steer away from them.

The "Kitchen Sink"

The kitchen sink concept is the one where the team throws in anything they can about the product or service because they view everything as equally important. Generally, this happens early in the concept-writing process, and the primary cause is a lack of clear thinking about the benefit(s) to be offered. Hence, the tendency is to throw everything into the concept, including the "kitchen sink." It becomes very difficult to develop a copy strategy for a concept like this because there's no single-minded focus from which to start. Only certain elements of the concept are likely to support any particular benefit.

The "Frankenconcept"

Tom Fishburne, a onetime classmate of mine at the Harvard Business School, has created a wealth of marketing and market research–related cartoons. I must credit Tom with the term "Frankenconcept," used in one of my favorite Brand Camp cartoons:

Used with Permission—Tom Fishburne

The "Frankenconcept" evolves later in the concept-writing process than the "kitchen sink" because it is generally a combination of average concepts. The outcome, however, is much the same as the "kitchen sink" in that the lack of a single-minded focus makes the development of a copy strategy impossible.

Outside the footprint/brand equity

When developing line extensions or "flankers," sometimes the team gets very excited about innovation and begins to move too far away from the brand's core equity or footprint. It's important to understand from a *consumer* perspective just how far the brand can be stretched and still be relevant. Even though the management team believes that the brand can move into new territory, the extensions need to fit into a set of considerations acceptable to the consumer. For example, if you have a brand that competes primarily in the foot-care category, it might make complete sense to introduce new products for the hands—but not for eye care. Because hands and feet generally get a lot of wear and tear, soothing products are applied on the surface of the skin. The efficacy of these products, however, may not provide consumers with the confidence that something applied in the eye would be safe. Another example might be a cleaning product that is identified with mildness or gentleness trying to make hard-hitting claims like "effective in seconds" or "deeply penetrates the fabric." These claims sound too aggressive to fit with the brand identity.

Line extension of a weak brand name

In order to extend a brand, the "mother brand" must have strong credibility and already own a specific place in the consumer's mind. Even though it is almost always easier to get a new sale from an existing buyer than to start from scratch with a new customer, the base can't sustain a new addition without a strong foothold in the market. Sometimes, testing an idea with and without the brand name can identify how much value the brand adds. If the branded positioning concept doesn't add any value to the credibility or interest in the proposition, then you probably don't have a viable line-extension positioning concept.

A "me too"

A "me too" happens when you are late to market and jump in to get a piece of the pie. This usually won't work, even if you have a superior offering. The product that got to the market first with a key benefit generally wins. For example, in October 2010, the Amazon Kindle virtually owned the e-book market, with an estimated 76 percent of the U.S. market. Other e-readers hardly had a chance; not only were they late to the market, but also the Kindle was linked to Amazon, an established distribution point for the brand and one with consumer credibility. It wasn't until the Apple iPad entered the market with a new and different way to serve up e-books that Amazon began to feel some competitive pain.[4] Although competition may increase as downloading books becomes easier, Kindle has remained strong because it was first to the market.

Unique, but irrelevant benefit vs. competition

Creativity can get the best of you. The momentum behind innovation can lead you to make some extraordinary promises, but the consumer may not be interested. Generally, this means that you didn't do your homework thoroughly enough before you developed your concept—and, as a result, your development process wasn't driven by consumer learning. When you take a concept that results from this setup into a quantitative concept test, you may get high scores for uniqueness but miss your purchase-intent goals. Here's a made-up example to illustrate my point:

---

4   Alex Pham, "Amazon Is Ready to Jump into the Next Chapter with Its Kindle" (*Cleveland.com*, January 8, 2011, http://www.cleveland.com/business/index.ssf/2011/01/amazons_vision_for_the_kindle.html, accessed January 18, 2011).

When I'm at the drive-through window, it bothers me that I have to buy a large soda when I am thirsty, when the smaller sizes have unlimited refills if I sit in the restaurant.

Introducing the new soda Mega Jug—all the thirst-quenching enjoyment you want, in one giant cup.

Each Mega Jug holds 64 ounces of your favorite beverage for the same price as a refillable small size. You'll never be thirsty on the road again!

In theory, this proposition seems to fill certain unmet needs. And yes, the cup is probably relatively unique vs. other fast-food options. However, the purchase intent is probably low. Just imagine what the consumer is thinking:

- Why do I need two quarts of soda in a cup?
- How am I going to fit that in my cup holder in the car?
- How am I going to lift that cup with one hand? Does it have two handles?
- If it has two handles, how do I drive?

As you see, uniqueness and purchase intent don't necessarily move in the same direction.

The finish line is about adding all of the important elements beyond the ACB, benefit, and RTB to the positioning concept in order to complete the communication. Basically, you want to wrap the concept up with a bow, just like a present. The positioning concept is at the center, and the wrapping paper, bow, and tag make it a gift that is ready for further testing.

KEY THINGS TO REMEMBER:

- ✓ Keep the headline focused on the benefit, and don't add new benefits.
- ✓ Make the headline memorable, but not an advertisement.
- ✓ Use different words in the summary—the wrap-up—that imply the same thing as the benefit-focused headline.
- ✓ Add the other essential information only after you've reached the core idea for the consumer.
- ✓ Avoid the classic pitfalls: the "kitchen sink" concept, the Frankenconcept, getting too far from your brand equity, jumping into a market too late, or offering an irrelevant benefit.

CHAPTER 10

IMAGES AND VISUALS

"A picture is worth a thousand words."
—Unknown

The challenge with visuals is that an image that might spark the interest of one potential consumer might completely disengage another one. The subjective nature of this response means that careful thought must go into the choice of images.

This area should be more than just a necessary afterthought. It is critical to ensure that the image communicates *exactly* what you intend; otherwise, you might get a backlash.

DO I REALLY NEED AN IMAGE?

Whether an image is necessary depends on what stage of the process you are involved in, as well as whether the concept really needs a visual aid such as an illustration, film, or photograph to communicate the benefit.

In early positioning-concept development, a visual component is generally not necessary. The primary objective at this stage is to determine if you have a unique and ownable proposition that sparks some consumer interest.

For quantitative testing, you may want some type of visual to help communicate the positioning concept—to clarify a particular aspect of it. For example, when Apple iPhone applications were first introduced, actually seeing what was being communicated was very important. Now, because the market is well educated, these visuals are not as necessary.

If the written positioning concept clearly communicates the idea, you can skip the visual. In this case, the visual won't add anything to the positioning concept—in fact, if the visual is a poor fit with the idea, it may simply cause confusion. Don't add a visual just because "that's the way we always do it." Generally, common products such as detergents, bug killers, and toilet paper don't need visuals to get the initial point across.

I've just proposed the two bookends for inclusion of a visual; now you have to figure out when to introduce one and what visual to select. The image usually comes in *early* in the process in two areas:

- **A breakthrough idea.** This is any type of positioning concept where the "form" of the core idea doesn't have an anchor point with the consumer. Some technology, engineering, or design offerings might fall into this area. Tech examples include the iPhone, a netbook, or an e-reader such as the Kindle. Engineering and design examples include hybrid cars, the Concorde airplane, the Dyson vacuum—and something as simple a new brush structure or shape for a toothbrush. Important: Make sure that your words fully communicate the message in the picture so, when your concept translates to advertising, the words there can paint that picture as clearly as possible.

- **A mood-board visual.** This is generally a collage or montage of pictures that communicates the tonality of the positioning. Think of a new shampoo. If the shampoo is positioned as natural, with a citrus scent, a mood board might capture the essence of this idea with a visual of a natural outdoor scene with fresh orange and lime slices. By contrast, if the shampoo were positioned as a product to repair damaged hair with vitamins, then the visual would look completely different. While the use of a mood board is really at the discretion of the marketer, it can be very helpful in a crowded or cluttered category where differentiation is difficult to achieve. Two key areas of importance: Make sure that you prepare a variety of mood boards to ensure that you've covered all possible areas of interest. The client or agency tends to pick a "winner" before the development process begins—and this can bias results. By showing a wide cross-section of options from which the consumer

can select, not just the management's favorite, you
can ensure that you haven't led the consumer to a
mediocre positioning. Second, make sure the mood
boards are approachable and relevant to the average
consumer; sometimes an agency board can get a bit
too artsy and ethereal for a consumer to understand.

Other visuals can be introduced later in the development process, though this can sometimes be tricky. As
noted earlier, a visual should be included only if it is critical
in communicating the concept. Going back to our hair-care
example, if you have products that help make hair shine,
capturing this sheen might underscore the product benefit.

If you are going to visually showcase the benefit, then
don't be cheap! If you decide to put in a simple artist's illustration or a poor-quality photo, you may fail to capture
the beauty of the hair. If you really believe that you need
a visual, then you need to invest the time and money to do
it right.

Assuming that you decide to move forward with a visual,
a good time to add it is after you've nailed down your lead
positioning concepts. I would strongly suggest that you test
these qualitatively, just to be sure that you've got it right,
before moving into a quantitative test. You do not want a
good idea to score poorly in quantitative testing because
you have the wrong visual.

Let me relate a quick story to illustrate my point. I was
working on a new concept for some dairy products. An element of the concept related to organic farms in Vermont.
Naturally, the team felt that a nice spotted cow (a la Ben
& Jerry's) was the perfect visual. Wrong! While some consumers related to the cow, others said that they didn't really

want to think about their milk coming from a dirty cow out in a field. To further complicate matters, a whole discussion ensued about whether the cow should be brown and white, black and white, or a solid color.

The client was shocked, but we all got a good laugh out of it. Obviously, we showed no cow when the concept went on to quantitative testing!

Selecting the right picture(s)

These guidelines should help you find the right pictures for your positioning concepts. Generally speaking, the right picture:

- focuses on the end benefit. A positioning concept is all about having a "hook" that the consumer needs and/or wants. If you are claiming whiter teeth or straighter hair, then show it!
- is relevant to the target audience. If you have a product for both men and women, make sure your photo relates to both genders. While I do not intend to stereotype anyone, a visual that reads as pink, lacy, and flowery probably won't entice your male target. Similarly, showing hunting, fishing, or a tool shed likely won't appeal to most females.
- should depict somewhat accurate packaging. In consumer products, an image of the packaging and/or sizes should be at least somewhat accurate. Don't talk about breakthrough packaging if the package visual shown is a stock bottle! Similarly, if the brand is already known, don't mess around with the packaging equities (color, logo, etc.). That should be done in a different test, not a concept test.

For multiple concepts of the same product or service, it's critical to use:

- the same type and quality of image for all concepts—either all illustrations or all photos on all related concepts. You don't want someone to select a concept simply because its picture is more realistic, for example.
- the same color type for all concepts. Don't have some concepts in black and white and others in color. Similarly, the package(s) and graphics should be either all black and white or all color—not a mix.
- the same package(s) and graphics for all concepts. This is the not the venue for testing these elements, so just eliminate these from consideration.

The biggest issues with concept visuals and pictures are that they may:

- fit poorly with the positioning concept. This usually happens when the visual is placed on the whiteboard concept as an afterthought before quantitative testing. This mistake tends to fall into the category we mentioned earlier—"We always do it that way." But placing just any image on a concept can be self-defeating. For example, you don't want an image that doesn't fit with the benefit the consumer is evaluating in the concept. Even worse is to try to make the concept an advertisement with a visual that makes no sense without the context of full copy in a print ad. Either way, the consumer might evaluate the positioning concept based on something other than the primary driver, which should be the benefit.

- distract and/or overwhelm the positioning concept. This often occurs when the visuals get complicated, particularly when several images are layered together. While the creator of the montage may think it supports all of the concept's different aspects, it can overwhelm the written positioning concept and take the consumer in a different direction. The consumer may evaluate the images instead of the key message of the written concept.

- lack relevance to the target audience—skewed by gender or race. You want your concept to speak to your primary target. If the concept is supposed to have unisex appeal, then it is imperative that the images communicate that effectively without visuals that skew feminine or masculine. In terms of racial bias, if your product or service is meant for everyone, make sure the people in the visual are not all blond, blue-eyed, and size 6—that is not going to work! All the words in the world can't erase a visual that leads to either form of bias.

- try to communicate and/or educate too much. This usually happens when a marketer hasn't made the concept clear enough for consumer understanding. In such cases, the marketer perceives the picture as serving an educational role to augment the written concept. Such pictures usually do one of two things: show how to use the product—the picture sequence might look something like the exclusively visual directions for putting together a piece of IKEA furniture—or teach new information, when a marketer thinks the consumer might need additional context. If you feel the need to teach in your positioning concept, you probably have not explained the idea well enough.

Clearly, deciding on the need and selecting the actual visual should not be an afterthought. It requires time, consideration, and, often, money to develop a visual that builds and enhances your written concept communication. The image you choose can hurt or it can help; you just need to understand where it falls in this spectrum.

KEY THINGS TO REMEMBER:

- ✓ Determine if your positioning concept really needs an image in order to communicate the idea.
- ✓ If you select an image, make sure that you prequalify it with potential consumers to ensure that you have the right one before you pay for an expensive quantitative test.
- ✓ If you are testing multiple concepts for the same product, make sure that the image quality, type of image, color, and any graphics are fundamentally the same.

CHAPTER 11

QUALITATIVE RESEARCH

Qualitative and quantitative research each have a role in your concept-development and writing efforts. We'll explore each one individually; however, they can often be combined for optimal development and evaluation.

According to the Qualitative Research Consultants Association (QRCA):

> Qualitative research is designed to reveal a target audience's range of behavior and the perceptions that drive it with reference to specific topics or issues. It uses in-depth studies of small groups of people to guide and support the construction of hypotheses. The results of qualitative research are descriptive, rather than predictive.
>
> Qualitative methods include in-depth interviews with individuals, group discussions (from two to ten participants is typical); diary and journal exercises;

and in-context observations. Sessions may be conducted in person, by telephone, via videoconferencing, and via the Internet.

In the context of concept writing, qualitative research includes using your target audience to understand habits, practices, and motivations in the category. Qualitative research will also help you determine lead ideas, develop those ideas, and capture the consumer's true language to create your best possible concept.

Qualitative research for concept creation and optimization comes in various sizes and shapes. These can be in person or online, in groups or one-on-one. The chart below illustrates the strong and weak points of working with groups vs. one-on-one.

Qualitative interview approach

Weak/Low ✔   Strong/High ✔✔✔

	GROUP	ONE-ON-ONE
DISCUSSION BREADTH		
Lots of interactive discussion among respondents	✔✔✔	✔
Building/enhancing concept elements	✔✔✔	✔
In-depth discussion on interpretation	✔	✔✔✔
LANGUAGE		
Addressing many benefits/concepts	✔✔✔	✔
Communications check	✔✔	✔✔✔
IMAGES		
Optimizing image(s)	✔✔✔	✔

IN-PERSON QUALITATIVE RESEARCH

In-person qualitative research generally offers a great deal of time for discussion, with other respondents and/or the moderator. Having a group of respondents allows you to have breadth in your discussion and bring out many opinions. This can be very helpful in soliciting feedback in a variety of areas. The group—commonly called the focus group—creates a safe environment to solicit feedback. The dialogue among respondents can add a richness that can enable you to take your concept to a new level. Generally, in a qualitative setting, you want to work with a group of five to eight consumers.

One-on-one interviews or in-depth interviews (IDIs) are best used at the end of development as you hone in on the lead approaches. One-on-ones are helpful to ensure that all communication points are understood and that the logic makes sense.

A primary advantage of any in-person session is that it is a controlled environment; this ensures that your concept stimuli won't leave the research facility and get into the wrong hands.

ONLINE QUALITATIVE RESEARCH

Online research offers some distinct advantages over more traditional in-person qualitative research. Let's take a look:

- Online provides a more diverse demographic sample. Generally, our buyers of products and services are in a wide spectrum of locations—a few regions in the U.S., or around the world. Either way, the online approach can help link these consumers in the same discussion and allow a broader scope for comparing and contrasting experiences, wants, and needs. Of course, discussions must be conducted among people who speak the same language and have like-minded habits. But imagine the value of understanding how a person in the U.K. thinks about a concept compared with someone in Australia or the U.S. In addition, typing responses allows for "blinded accents" as well as twenty-four-hour feedback.

- Online allows for nearly constant, real-time collaboration with clients. The online approach allows the client to be intimately involved in the process. Being just a typed message away enables strong communication between the moderator/consultant and the client at virtually any time. The client simply logs in a few times a day to catch up on the new learning. This is particularly helpful when you have key client constituencies that can't leave the office for a week to attend working sessions for a concept effort. In addition to reading and contributing comments throughout the process, the consultant can leverage their knowledge with a scheduled conference call at the end of each day.

Online interviews can be done in real time or asynchronously (individuals can participate when it is convenient for them across several days and times). The real-time approach is often called a chat board or online chat. The asynchronous approach is called an online bulletin board (OLBB). An asynchronous bulletin board can be done as a group or as a one-on-one, depending on where you are in the development cycle.

Online bulletin boards vs. chat boards

An online bulletin board (OLBB) creates the unique ability to learn and build with the *same* consumer. An OLBB is typically structured for multiple days; I'll typically run an OLBB session for three to five consecutive days. This provides the opportunity to start with the basic learning about habits and practices and then develop a full concept as the clients participate over time. The huge benefit to the client team is that it will know immediately when it veers off course because the iterative nature of the concept-building process will quickly reveal the problems—and the clients already know how the earlier ideas played with the consumer. In addition, because the client is already "warmed up" by days two to five, rehashing baseline learning is not necessary. You can spend all of your time on augmenting the concept effort.

Extraordinarily fast feedback is among the advantages of a chat board. A group chat board occurs very rapidly because, unlike traditional, in-person groups, virtually everyone can "talk" at once; participants are limited only by their typing speed. You'll get abundant feedback, though it can be a bit more challenging to keep track of all of this feedback due to the rapid pace. Of course, you'll get a transcript at the end, but it can be difficult to answer follow-up questions because of the rapid gunfire hail of information.

I prefer OLBBs over online chat boards because the ability to think and type quickly is not a factor. In an OLBB, participants can reflect on the elements in the concept at their own speed; they don't need to keep up with a group.

Online alert

When you work over the Internet, you need to be aware that you cannot control the distribution of the information. Technology allows us to cut, paste, copy, grab, and save so easily that, even though you manage the time frame of online qualitative research, you can't ensure that your information won't be shared, even with a competitor.

QUAL BEFORE QUANT

The rush to get a new product or service developed and into the market sometimes puts a project team under both time and financial pressures. In these circumstances, a team may feel that they need to cut a few corners and take their concepts from idea directly to quantitative research (quant). This strategy of skipping qualitative research (qual) might save some time and money, but the danger is that a concept might underperform because it hasn't been vetted before the quantitative test. A round of qualitative work might prevent the loss of a great idea.

Here are some other dangers you can avoid by placing qualitative research first:

- **You're not using consumer/customer language.** We often forget that our target audience doesn't spend as much time thinking about the product as a typical brand manager does. Often, consumers have a simple reason for delighting in an offering. Unfortunately, concept-writing teams can get stuck in "manufacturer-speak." The language in the concept might convince management that you have a great offering, but potential buyers often reject concepts laden with "insider language" because such language does not speak to them in a relevant and personal way.

- **Your name choice is polarizing.** The name for the product that you and your team think is cute or transparent just might not be. Marketers and managers often overlook this concern. In reality, naming requires complex study and should be a separate effort for new product or service development. Names can be very polarizing because they mean different things to different people. The last thing you want to find out in your quant test is that you haven't gotten a fair read on your product or service because the name diminished the purchase intent.

- **The logic doesn't tie together.** The marketer and the R&D specialist understand the inner workings of a product or service. They are close to the development process and probably have spent more waking hours thinking about it than virtually anyone else on the planet. Unfortunately, what becomes common sense to the insiders may not be quite so obvious to the target audience. A round of qualitative research provides an objective review, ensuring that the concept isn't confusing and that the RTB is believable and delivers the promised benefit(s).

- **Your concept is too technical.** Generally, a concept needs to communicate the "big idea" to the end user, whether this individual is a consumer, a doctor, a CEO, or someone else. As knowledge experts, our tendency is to want to showcase how smart we are instead of simply to communicate a powerful idea. Intel provides us with a great example of how to communicate a compelling idea. A high-quality, high-performance computer chip may require a lot of complex engineering, but as end buyers, we've been educated simply that Intel stands for quality. As such, telling buyers that a computer has "Intel Inside" gives them confidence that their PC will work well. It's the KISS theory—"Keep it simple, silly." A round of qualitative research can help you adhere to this theory.

- **It's not single-minded.** As we have seen before, a common mistake is to tell a potential buyer *all* of the great qualities a product offers. While a positioning concept like this will test well in quant because it offers something for everyone, it will be impossible to deliver one compelling selling idea that will satisfy everyone who loved the concept. A round of qualitative research helps to ensure that you communicate only one idea—and that will make the job of delivering it much easier. In qualitative, if the question "What is the main idea?" gets many unique answers, the concept may test well in quant, but no one will know which main idea is the winner.

Optimizing the presentation order in qualitative research

One of the main challenges concept-development teams face is how to get unbiased consumer feedback. You want to be able to showcase a variety of concepts without each exposure influencing the future thinking on new ideas.

Most researchers would agree that you can't entirely eliminate this problem, but there are certain ways to minimize it. Here are six things to consider when researching multiple concepts; these will help you maintain objectivity with your target audience.

- Rotate the presentation order. Whether you're showing multiple concepts in an in-person or online forum, it's critical to rotate the order of the concepts. This way, you'll at least know that each concept is viewed first at some point; not only will this tell you that the respondents understand what they are reading, but it also allows you to gauge their interest level more easily.

- Ask individuals to rank each concept before they come together as a group. It is sometimes helpful to give each respondent a pack of concepts to read through before starting any group discussion. Ask respondents to rate the concept on a five-point scale and record their initial reaction. Alternatively, you can have them rank the concepts by preference or sort them into "Keep," "Throw," or "Improve" piles. In this scenario, it's critical that the moderator and the team pay close attention to the reason something ends up in a "Throw" pile. It might be fixable—so don't fall on your sword after this initial run-through. The key to success in this approach is to have each individual record his or her thoughts before hearing from others.

- Restructure group size. Another way to optimize qualitative testing is to employ many smaller consumer sessions early on. For example, try employing a group of three individuals to review only a couple of concepts instead of a group of eight people reviewing eight to ten concepts. You may find that you learn more in the triads because group fatigue and bias are minimized, allowing for fresher reactions to the ideas. In addition, you can tweak the concept with each iteration, thus enhancing the dynamic development process. At the end of the research, you may want to have a larger group do a final "disaster" check on the enhanced ideas, but at that point you aren't looking to enhance them further—you just want to make sure they work.

- Provide an activity between each concept. Sometimes a creative exercise between concepts can provide a breather to clear the participants' minds. This can be as simple as a "toss the ball" or a "picture pick" exercise. Bear in mind that this approach might be easiest with a fun group of respondents and a moderator with an engaging style. A somber moderator dealing with a serious topic would probably deem this inappropriate.

- Go online. Finally, consider moving your project to an online bulletin board. In this venue, you can set up interviews on one board where the participants may or may not interact with one another. Several simultaneous bulletin boards would enable you to rotate the order of the concepts. If you want some time between each exposure, you can set up the boards over several days, showing only one or two concepts each day. This way, the respondents will bring a fresh perspective to the ideas on each visit.

With this method, four sessions of fifteen to twenty minutes each might prove more fruitful than spending one hour on the bulletin board for one day.

- Employ nonleading identifiers. It is much easier to keep track of your concepts with your consumer if you give each concept a unique identifier. This helps with the presentation order as well as later discussions. However, it's important to keep the identifiers as neutral as possible. Here are a couple rules of thumb:

  - Don't use numbers—ranking numbers is difficult because our brains naturally want to put numbers in order; just don't use them and you won't have this problem.

  - Keep identifiers nonsequential—when using letters, pick random letters like P, Q, V, and X so there is no perceived order. If the order is X-Y-Z, for example, people will tend to rank them in the same way they tend to order numbers.

  - Use letters, preferably consonants only—in the American alphabet, we are lucky enough to have twenty-six unique identifiers, which is generally enough for your concepts. I'd advise you to skip the vowels, simply because when you ask a respondent to rank the letters, you don't want them to spell a word like "stink" (or something worse!) when you write letters on a flip chart.

  - Avoid rhyming—for the sake of those listening in the back room and for the moderator, try to avoid the letters that rhyme, because they start to sound the same—B, C, G, P, T, and V, for example. If you have to, move to double letters such as BB or SS because they will sound different.

- Avoid letters with loaded meaning—while I don't view this as essential, if you have the luxury of not needing all 21 consonants, then drop the ones associated with school grades: A, B, C, D, and F. (Of course, you already should have knocked "A" out of consideration because it's a vowel.)

Iterative qualitative research

A different way to leverage the power of qualitative research is to create your concepts iteratively over a period of time—usually a week. To conduct iterative qualitative research, select your primary target and schedule six to ten back-to-back research sessions over a few days. These research sessions often benefit from a combination of methodologies including focus groups, triads, one-on-ones, and in-context. The target, however, needs to stay stable so that you gain cumulative learning from the consumer over the time period. The key to a successful process is a committed team that will stay engaged for the entire research period. You also will need smart scheduling to allow for rework and rethinking.

When performing iterative research, you begin with the benefit and then add the other elements, one at a time. The advantage of building the full concept in this step-by-step manner is that you can ensure that each element is clear, logical, and relevant before you add extra information. Often consumers will get hung up in the "why"—the RTB—which can make it difficult for them to focus on the rest of the concept. Therefore, it's imperative that your targets first understand your benefit—what you are offering them—before you introduce any more-distracting elements. When you employ iterative research, the client team has a chance to hear real-time feedback as each new element is added and make adjustments accordingly.

Another key benefit of the iterative process is that you create team unity around an optimized concept. The process can help rally enthusiasm and support for the optimized approach. The process encourages a lone voice to raise a concern that can be "tested"—and then either embraced or abandoned. At the end, no one can say they weren't responsible or really wanted something else. That "something else" will have had its day. There is no better way to gain team alignment when developing concepts.

Iterative qualitative work also can help you avoid an expensive quant test on a lackluster concept. With an iterative approach, the work that precedes quantitative research ensures the best possible inputs. Of course, upfront optimization in iterative research costs money, but that is nothing compared with a quantitative test that doesn't deliver the desired output. If the product does not meet quantitative purchase-intent criteria—the total percentage of respondents who state that they "will definitely buy" or "will probably buy," set at the project start—you will need to start over and spend even more money and effort on development. You would likely prefer to spend that time and money on bringing the product to market, not on rework.

Now that you've qualitatively maximized your consumer understanding and optimized your positioning concept with small groups of consumers, it's time to think about quantitative testing. Not all companies test quantitatively, but it is generally a good practice; it will confirm that your product has the broad-scale appeal and purchase intent that will help drive its eventual success in the marketplace.

KEY THINGS TO REMEMBER:

- ✓ Determine what type of qualitative research will best suit your needs, keeping in mind who your consumer is, the nature of the topic, and your project timing.
- ✓ Some qualitative research should always be done before you field a quantitative test so that you can identify and address any problems before you spend money on the test.
- ✓ Make sure that you get consumer feedback that is as unbiased as possible by optimizing the presentation order of the concept.
- ✓ Consider iterative qualitative research to optimize each element of your positioning concepts before you add incremental information.

CHAPTER 12

QUANTITATIVE RESEARCH*

In contrast to qualitative research, quantitative research focuses on a broader audience. At this point, you'll be putting your entire "final" concept, with or without an image, into the next evaluation step. Your concept will probably look more like the concept for the 4KidsOnly cell phone that you read about in chapter 4.

The term quantitative research is defined by the website BusinessDirectory.com as the "use of sampling techniques (such as consumer surveys) whose findings may be expressed numerically, and are amenable to mathematical (statistical) manipulation enabling the researcher to estimate (forecast) future events or quantities."

In designing the quantitative concept test, there are a variety of things to consider, many of which are interrelated. This makes the design of a quantitative test somewhat

*Written with help from Linda Marholin, Quantum Insights

iterative, which will become clearer as we discuss the various design elements. These elements are:

- methodology
- sampling
- questionnaire design
- analysis

METHODOLOGY: HOW SHOULD YOU COLLECT THE DATA?

There are many ways to collect the data. The three most commonly used methodologies for quantitative concept tests are online, telephone, and in person. Each one has strengths and weaknesses. In deciding which one to employ, you will need to consider the other design elements of the study, such as sampling.

Online interviewing has several advantages. First, it allows you to collect a lot of data in a short amount of time at a very reasonable cost. In addition, you can show respondents rather lengthy concepts as well as ones that include pictures or graphics. You will need to make sure that your desired target is reachable in an online modality and that you can get accurate, up-to-date e-mail addresses. Also, it can sometimes be difficult to validate that the person taking the study is actually the target you recruited. One way to minimize this problem is to employ more-intricate screening questions to weed out inappropriate respondents right before they have access to the questionnaire.

Telephone is probably still the strongest methodology in terms of sampling and control. The majority of the population can still be reached by telephone. One advantage to this method is that a trained interviewer can encourage cooperation and reduce confusion while collecting all necessary data. The biggest drawback to using the telephone for concept tests is that you need to limit the length of the concepts. Keep in mind that the concepts will have to be read to the respondents and that there is an upper limit to the amount of information they can process in this way. Another disadvantage is that telephone studies can be costly.

In-person interviews allow you to lay out longer concepts to respondents and include pictures, graphics, and objects. Generally, this approach is required if the respondent must see or taste a product. In addition, interviews can optimize the benefits of a trained interviewer. The downsides are the limits to the geographic coverage of the study, and the costs—interviews can be fairly costly to execute.

Quantitative interview approaches

Weak/Low ✔   Strong/High ✔✔✔

	TELEPHONE	ONLINE	IN-PERSON
TARGET AUDIENCE			
Ease of finding	✔✔✔	✔	✔✔
Reach largest population	✔✔✔	✔✔	✔
Geographic coverage	✔✔✔	✔✔✔	✔

	TELEPHONE	ONLINE	IN-PERSON
WRITTEN STIMULI			
Can read concept	N/A	✔✔✔	✔✔✔
Can hear concept	✔✔✔	N/A	✔✔✔
Longer concepts	✔	✔✔✔	✔✔✔
Higher number of concepts	✔✔	✔✔	✔✔✔
NONWRITTEN STIMULI			
Show images	N/A	✔✔✔	✔✔✔
Show objects	N/A	N/A	✔✔✔
TRAINED INTERVIEWER			
Able to use	✔✔✔	N/A	✔✔✔
TIMING			
Quicker completion	✔✔	✔✔✔	✔
COST			
Economical	✔	✔✔✔	✔
CONFIDENTIALITY			
Control of stimuli	✔✔✔	✔	✔✔✔

SAMPLING: WHOM DO YOU NEED TO TALK TO?

Sampling design is more than just a simple matter of whom we need to talk to. Among the complicated details that are part of this question:

- Do I need to include different target audiences? If so, how many?
- How many completed interviews do I need?
- What qualifying characteristics must they have (are they within a specific age range, do they have to participate in a specific behavior, and so on)?
- Where can I find this audience (at home, at work)?
- What is their geographic footprint?
- How do I find the desired target audience?
- What modality is the best for a particular target audience: phone, Internet, or in person?

Once you have figured out the answers to these questions, you need to find a reliable source for phone numbers or e-mail addresses. Sometimes these can be found inside your organization; at other times, you may need to purchase a sample.

QUESTIONNAIRE DESIGN: WHAT DO YOU NEED TO ASK?

Quantitative concept tests can be set up to test whole concepts, individual benefits, or a combination of the two. The structure of the questionnaire is based on the objectives of the study as well as the number, length, and type of concepts to be tested. This structure will also affect the sampling design, especially in terms of the number of interviews that need to be completed.

When testing multiple concepts, you will need to decide if it is better to test them monadically or sequential-monadically. In a monadic design, each respondent sees only one concept; this requires that your sample design include multiple cells of statistically identical respondents. Some researchers prefer this approach because it is much closer to what happens in a real environment. When using a sequential monadic design, each respondent sees multiple concepts, one at a time; this can reduce or eliminate the need for multiple cells of respondents. This approach also allows for more discrimination among concepts. The choice of approach is not entirely academic; the type of concepts being tested, the objectives of the study, the budget, and the sensitivity of the research will determine which design to choose.

	ADVANTAGES	DISADVANTAGES
Monadic	• More like what happens in the real world	• Need multiple cells of statistical respondents • Can become expensive
Sequential monadic	• Eliminates need for multiple cells of statistical respondents • More cost efficient	• More discrimination among concepts

Just as in qualitative research, you will need to rotate the concepts to reduce order bias.

When designing your concept test, it's important to ensure that your questions are written clearly, focused on the objectives, and unbiased. You will want to be sure to include rating questions for your concepts and/or benefits, as well as for the all-important purchase-intent question. These questions should be designed with a consistent scale that offers the right level of variation and anchoring for your needs.

ANALYSIS: HOW DO YOU SLICE AND DICE THE DATA?

Now that you have collected your data, how do you know if your concept is going to produce the results you want in the marketplace? What is the decision factor that will determine your "go/no go" decision? The possible decision factors depend on how your concept test is designed. This means that you will need to think through your analysis plan before completing your questionnaire or finalizing your sampling plan. Some decision factors may be based simply on a top box score from the scale in the purchase-intent question. Others are far more complex and involve multivariate techniques that encompass the responses from a variety of questions.

Norms are an interesting and useful tool. They can be very helpful in deciding whether or not to move ahead with a concept. Norms are developed from the performance of other concepts in quantitative testing. These other concepts can provide bases for comparison and help you to predict how well your concept will perform in the marketplace. There are two basic types of norms: internal and external.

Internal norms are developed within a company using only that company's data. Internal norms can be particularly helpful if the products (upon which the norms were created) were launched *and* matched the concept description. In this instance, the organization can compare concept reaction to performance.

External norms are usually developed by consulting companies that gather data across companies and often across industries. Generally, external norms are desired even though it may be harder to find reliable comparisons.

Which type of norms, if any, will serve you best depends on a variety of factors that include what industry you are in, how similar or different your company is to the competition, and whether you designed your concept test to be comparable to a specific norm.

Volume estimation is another type of analysis that can be used to assess the viability of your concept. In order to implement this type of analysis, you will need to include specific questions in your questionnaire; these questions must provide data that will enable you to estimate the volume of the product that could be sold.

Foremost, all of the concept test design elements need to address the goals and objectives of the study. After that, you need to select a methodology, sampling plan, questionnaire design, and analysis plan that together work to achieve those goals and objectives.

Overall, it's important to remember that both qualitative and quantitative research play an important part in your building and qualification process. Your core team needs to address and agree on the appropriate protocol and the evaluation criteria before you start any research. It's hard to know if you've achieved your success criteria if the team hasn't agreed on what those milestones are in each phase of the research.

KEY THINGS TO REMEMBER:

✓ Know your business objectives and budget before you select an approach.

✓ Understand the choices in four key areas—methodology, sampling, questionnaire design, and analysis—when working with your research provider.

CHAPTER 13

DIFFERENT AUDIENCES

I often hear statements like these from my clients:

- "But my customer is different than a typical consumer, so my concept should be structured differently."
- "Compared to others, we have to put a huge amount of detail in our concepts."
- "We sell to two different audiences, and we should have completely different concepts for each."

Generally, these statements are not accurate. Remember, we're talking about positioning concepts here. A positioning concept finds a home for your product in the consumer's mind. It is *not* about communicating everything that your product or service can offer to anyone who might possibly consider buying it. Fundamentally, every positioning concept must have the basic elements we've already discussed: accepted consumer belief (ACB), benefit, and reason to believe (RTB). If it doesn't have these elements, then you don't have a concept ready to be considered for *any* type of communication strategy—over and out!

The key is always to understand the distribution method used and the person making the decisions. You need to consider what audience you are addressing: business to consumer (B2C), business to business (B2B), and business to intermediary. Let's briefly explore each one.

BUSINESS TO CONSUMER (B2C)

This embraces all the stuff that you (the reader) might consider purchasing. If you've seen and/or heard an ad, received a flyer, gotten a coupon, seen a shelf tag, gotten a promotional gadget with a logo and selling line, received direct mail or e-mail—you name it—this is where it's at. A business is selling something to an end consumer—and that's you. Consumers generally make purchase decisions based on comfort, quality, status (brand), or security.

Think about it. For every purchase you make, you have a conscious reason for the selection. It doesn't matter if it is mayonnaise, a brand of clothes, a new bank account, or auto insurance—at some point you make a selection based on one reason or another. Whether that reason is flavor, quality, interest rate, or low cost, each of these choices differentiated itself in some way that you preferred. That's because something about the concept appealed to you. Consumer purchases tend to be much more emotional than those of a business buyer. As a result, a B2C positioning concept is likely to be less complicated. It will pinpoint those emotional triggers and the key drivers to persuade a consumer to make a purchase decision.

Netflix provides a good example. Basically, the company has helped drive the major bricks-and-mortar video rental stores into bankruptcy with a simple yet state-of-the-art delivery method with exceptional value. While the original concept focused on DVDs ordered online and delivered by mail for a monthly fee, their most recent concept move has focused on leveraging the downloading abilities of the Internet. Based on their website, the B2C concept probably reads something like this:

Hassle-free movies, anytime

I want to watch movies and TV shows when I feel like it. The last thing I want to do is drive to pick one up—or, worse, not be able to get the one I want.

Now with Netflix, you can instantly watch as many movies as you want without the hassle.

For a set monthly fee, simply download your favorite movies or TV episodes directly to your PC or Mac, or to your TV through a gaming system or Internet-ready DVD/Blu-ray system.

BUSINESS TO BUSINESS (B2B)

B2B involves any services or goods that are sold to other companies to operate. In this case, the "consumer" is a buyer in another company. The government, manufacturers, nonprofits, and resellers are the most common types of B2B markets. Typically, business buyers make purchase decisions for enhanced productivity, improved profitability, and reduced costs. This different mind-set will shape a positioning concept in a different way.

A B2B positioning concept still needs to work within the framework we've previously discussed, including ACB, benefit, and RTB. The key difference is that the RTB is likely to be more focused on information that will help a buyer make a strictly rational, rather than emotional, purchase decision. The concept must build credibility around its promise regardless of whether it is material or service oriented. The marketer must totally understand what motivates the buyer in order to reinforce his rational decision.

Here is an example of a concept that appeals solely to reason.

Foodies Just-in-Time (JIT) delivery: for fresh perishables every day

I work closely with college kitchen staff to ensure that we have the food they've ordered when they need it to meet their planned menu. However, sometimes keeping the perishables fresh can be a challenge.

Now, the new Foodies JIT delivery option ensures the freshest fruits and vegetables each and every day for less spoilage.

The JIT system allows the kitchen staff to select and specify delivery for all their perishables up to 24 hours in advance of delivery. Foodies guarantees delivery within a one-hour window of your desired delivery time.

BUSINESS TO INTERMEDIARY TO "END CUSTOMER"

This last type of concept often becomes two closely related concepts. The ultimate "end customer" should drive the primary concept communication; however, the intermediary needs to buy in to the concept at some level because it is the intermediary's job to sell the product or service. This "business" intermediary could come in the form of a wholesaler, distributor, broker, medical care provider, or procurement personnel. I'm using "business" as a collective term that also includes medical doctors, who are in the business of helping people get well, as well as more traditional business roles.

In each of these cases, the intermediary concept is likely to appear more robust than the end consumer concept because the intermediary likely needs more specifics. The end-customer concept may appear to be a "pullout"—that is, it may look like the most effective part of the concept was pulled out of the bigger concept. In reality, however, the customer concept is usually created first. The cleanest, simplest concept will target the end customer, and additional information will then be added to clinch the deal with the business intermediary.

The doctor/patient scenario is a perfect example. Now that many prescribed drugs are advertised directly to the consumer, an entirely new communication area has opened up to drug marketers. One example is the "purple pill"—Nexium, for heartburn relief. The website focuses on the patient need and cleverly wraps the color identification for memorability. While I don't know the exact positioning concept for the product when it was first developed, I can make an educated guess based on the website.

Possible patient concept:

The nighttime heartburn relief you need

During the day, I can use over-the-counter tablets for my heartburn, but at night when I lie down, the symptoms are unbearable. I can't find the relief I need.

Now try Nexium. It helps provide relief for acid reflux symptoms, both day and night.

Available only by prescription, Nexium is proven to treat acid reflux disease, which typically includes persistent heartburn on more than one day a week. You can find relief even when other treatments and dietary changes have proven ineffective. Nexium has no generic equivalent.

While this information is more than adequate to pique the patient's interest in the product, the concept for the doctor will need to be much more detailed because he has to know more than the patient about the chemistry of the drug.

Possible doctor concept:

Nighttime heartburn relief for your patients

During the day, my patients often rely on OTC tablets for heartburn, but at night when they lie down, the symptoms are often unbearable.

Now you can prescribe Nexium. It helps provide relief for acid reflux symptoms for your patients, both day and night.

Nexium is a protein pump inhibitor indicated for treating gastroesophageal reflux disease and reducing the risk of NSAID-associated gastric ulcer, and for reduction of *H. pylori* to reduce the risk of duodenal ulcer recurrence. Long-term usage may be associated with increased risk of osteoporosis. Nexium has no generic equivalent.

Of course, a doctor will need to know more details on dosing, reactions, warnings, and other things, but remember that doctors are hard to reach. The pharmaceutical representative tries to slip in between patient appointments with his branded pen, paper leave-behinds, and some samples. But often he will have to deal with aggressive receptionists: "No one sees my boss!" This means that a drug rep must have a very quick elevator speech that can communicate the essence of the drug he is selling in less than two minutes. Honestly, that isn't much longer than a thirty-second TV commercial. In my example, you'll note that the benefit is fundamentally the same, but the degree of explanation in the RTB is much more robust in the doctor concept.

Overall, the concepts are structured in the same way, but the person receiving the message will determine the amount of detail the target audience or the intermediary selling to an ultimate audience requires. In addition, when you are not selling directly to your end consumer, the voice must be adjusted to reflect the relationship of the "middle man" to the end consumer. You'll note in the previous example that the first-person singular, employed to speak directly to the consumer, is altered to refer to "my patient" in the doctor-focused approach; nevertheless, the benefit is the same to the ultimate purchaser.

So, once again, the power of science vs. art in writing a concept is clear. The science shows us that the format of a concept is essentially the same, no matter what the context may be. The art is in developing a level of detail and an understanding of who plays what role in the sales process.

KEY THINGS TO REMEMBER:

✓ Understand the audience you are addressing and where that audience fits in the sales cycle.

✓ Make sure that the benefit appeals to the ultimate end buyer, even if that purchase does not come directly from his wallet.

CHAPTER 14

HIRING AN EXPERT

Although many talented marketing and R&D professionals bring expert knowledge to their brands and organizations, some have not had the luxury of developing strong concept-writing skills. Often, this results from their companies not investing in the necessary training for employees. This is especially true for companies that hire trained expertise from outside companies. If that hired talent wasn't trained in his first job, the likelihood that he will learn concept writing in his next job is fairly low.

CONCEPT-WRITING EXPERT

Since strong concept writing skills are a rare commodity, clients can often gain substantial value by involving a trained concept writer and coach who can bring this much-needed expertise to the table. Working with a trained outsider can benefit an organization in four specific ways:

- **An objective eye**—an outsider brings the necessary objective eye to your business. A consultant can view your offerings more like a consumer than a seller or marketer can; this means that she can easily let your team know if they are being meaningful and relevant. Clients are often so immersed in their own business that they lose touch with a typical product or service interaction. Some clients believe that you need a researcher with industry expertise to work with your business, but I would disagree. If your consultant is too entrenched in all aspects of your business, he may not have the objectivity that your efforts require.

- **Understanding of structure**—one of the most common challenges for clients is to get their ideas on paper in a way that facilitates constructive feedback. Clients might leave a brainstorming session bursting with ideas, but they may not know how to determine if the ideas are winners. By contrast, the trained concept writer can ensure that the client's ideas are crisply communicated and that all the concept elements are balanced and flow logically from a consumer standpoint. But as basic as a concept framework is, most clients can't resist the temptation to keep on adding—until they ultimately lose track of the framework from which they started.

- **Speaking the target's language**—although many professionals may understand the fundamentals of a concept, translating that into consumer-relevant language is much more challenging than most people realize. I recently worked with a client on some concept development. Even though we had eight to ten ACBs to write, someone said, "We'll be out of here in an hour." Four hours later, we were still hard at work—though we had winning language when we finished. As much as we'd like to think that writing is easy, the simplicity and elegance of a written concept takes hard work. A consultant or coach who does this kind of work all the time is more keyed in to the cadence and rhythm of language that brings a sparkle to your consumers' eyes. This does *not* mean, however, that you should employ a copywriter. Concepts are not copy, so skip the advertising lingo!

- **Proactively identify problems**—because research is very expensive, anything that can be resolved *before* you spend money listening to consumer feedback is clearly cash back into your market-research budget. A trained concept writer can identify the obvious problems in your concept. These can be myriad: too many benefits, no benefit, no strong reason to believe the promise, or a confusing offering—to name just a few. I've seen a lot of concepts in my day, and I know that both large and small companies can fall into the same development traps. Having someone to coach you in solving the problems early will only enhance your development process.

QUALITATIVE MODERATOR WITH STRONG CONCEPT SKILLS

Even though you may have a favorite moderator for your business, when you embark on any qualitative research process to develop or refine your concepts, you will need a moderator who is an expert on effective positioning concepts. The concept-savvy moderator:

- **asks the right questions.** A moderator who works in the arena of concept development most of the time is very familiar with concept structure. She also knows the client needs to create a concept that translates well into a copy strategy. This knowledge enables her to ask the right questions—and to recognize helpful answers that will improve the concept.

- **hears concept language opportunities from respondents.** Similarly, an expert moderator is adept at listening for the right language to retool a concept. When she hears certain words from a consumer, she can effortlessly flip an insight into ACB language because she comes to the process from an objective place. In addition, she'll hear the small nuances that will help the concept communicate the desired message more tightly and clearly.

- **helps with the adjustments.** A talented moderator hears the language and can adjust or tweak language in real time with groups. This moves the concept refinement process forward more quickly and enables learning about potential changes before reworking the concept with the client.

- **helps eliminate order bias and respondent fatigue.**
  An expert moderator has the skills to realize when
  issues such as bias and fatigue crop up. Although
  the suggestions in chapter 11 address these issues, it
  always helps when your moderator is seasoned and
  skilled at dealing with these concerns in real time.

QUANTITATIVE RESEARCHER WITH STRONG CONCEPT TEST SKILLS

Conducting reliable quantitative concept tests can be
tricky. You will want to select a quantitative researcher
who knows how to integrate the right combination of
design elements—methodology, sampling, questionnaire
design, and analysis—to meet the objectives of the study. A
concept-knowledgeable quantitative expert:

- **selects the right methodology.** A quantitative expert
  knows how to balance the pros and cons of the various methodologies with the study objectives, the
  types of concepts to be tested, the target audience,
  and any budget constraints.

- **understands the complexities of sample design.** An
  expert can design a sampling plan that incorporates
  the right audience in the right numbers to fulfill any
  necessary quotas and provide actionable and project-
  able data. Such an expert will have a strong understanding of sample matching and weighting and
  knows where to obtain the desired sample.

- **asks the right questions.** An expert knows the types of questions to ask to elicit the data needed for the selected analysis. She also has the ability to write questions that are clear and unbiased.

- **provides the appropriate analysis.** A quantitative expert has a thorough knowledge of the various analysis options available and can apply them appropriately to predict accurately the level of success of the concepts in the marketplace.

You should first carefully evaluate the know-how inside your organization. This will enable you to recognize the areas where you might need outside expertise. Bringing in a knowledgeable person can be particularly helpful if you are severely time-constrained. These outside experts can streamline certain parts of the process and help you and your core team reach your goals more quickly and effectively.

CHAPTER 15

I'VE GOT MY CONCEPT; NOW WHAT?

So now you have a qualified lead concept for your offering. Congratulations! You've worked really hard to get to this place. You'll now use this concept to develop a copy (or advertising) strategy for your brand, product, or service. While the concept is used to identify the winning approach, the copy strategy is used to execute a desirable positioning. The diagram on the following page illustrates the relationship. The copy strategy will be the backbone of all of your communications—advertising, PR, sales and promotion sales material, website, endorsements, and any others.

The concept serves as one of the four building blocks in developing an effective copy strategy. In addition to the concept, the copy strategy includes the target audience, the brand character, and the purpose of the advertising.

As depicted above, the concept is defined as a promise (the benefit) and how that promise is supported (the reason to believe). The obvious question is, what happens to the accepted consumer belief (ACB)? In the process of developing a concept, the ACB serves as the contextual anchor that determines if there is a need, frustration, or problem to be solved. In addition, it sets the tonality for the concept—and this tonality will influence the development of the copy.

Below, I've included an example of a positioning concept so you can see the progression from concept to copy strategy.

Positioning concept

Brand X for dry, yet delicate protection

I really want to keep my baby as dry as possible, but some diapers give him a rash.

Now, improved Brand X disposable diaper provides effective protection while being gentle on the skin. That's because this new disposable diaper combines a unique bi-dry core that traps liquid, plus a soft, clothlike covering both inside and outside the diaper.

Brand X—the protection you need, the gentleness you want.

Example of copy strategy

Advertising will convince mothers of children under three years of age that caring mothers choose Brand X disposable diapers because they want effective protection that is also gentle on their baby's skin.

Only Brand X has a unique bi-dry core that traps liquid, plus a soft, clothlike covering both inside and outside the diaper.

Brand X's character: nurturing, smart, and warm.

As you can see, the copy strategy utilizes both the benefit and the RTB, then adds the elements of target audience and brand character (sometimes called "footprint" or "equity") to the mix. Many elements of the concept were carried over to the copy strategy.

So, there you have it. We've gone from preconcept to copy-ready in a mere fifteen chapters. I hope this book will serve as a constant reference tool for you during any of your new concept-development efforts. The tips and techniques here have worked for all of my many clients—and can work for you, too.

Now it's your turn. Good luck!

Trademarked Names Used Throughout This Book

Amazon Kindle
American Heart Association
Apple iPad
Apple iPhone
Apple iPod
Apple MacBook Air
AT&T
Ben & Jerry's
Blockbuster Video
Cascade
Chanel
Coca-Cola
Coke
Disney
Ford
Geico
Halls
Honda
IBM Selectric
Mentho-Lyptus
Monsanto
Netflix
Nexium
Nike

Olay Regenerist
Pantene
Pepsi
Polaroid
Pringles
Procter & Gamble
Raid
Restasis
Ritz Carlton
Rogaine
Roundup
Smart Car
Smucker's
Spray 'n Wash
Suave
Super Bowl
Trident
Tylenol
Vapor Action
Verizon
Volvo
Weight Watchers
Woolite

INDEX

WORKS CONSULTED

Dianne Altman-Weaver, "Good Ideas Gone Bad: Don't Rush Through Concept Execution" (*Marketing Research*, 2006).

Gary Burchill and Christina Hepner Brodie, "Voices into Choices: Acting on the Voice of the Customer" (Madison: Center for Quality of Management, 2005).

Larry A. Huston, "The Wealth Creation Power of a Concept" (speech, Cincinnati, OH, February 6, 1995).

Barbara Lippert, "Campaign of the Decade: Apple, 'Get a Mac'" (*Adweek,* 2010, http://www.bestofthe2000s.com/campaign-of-the-decade.html).

Charles M. Mayo and Deborah Hausler, "New Product Development," in *Reference For Business* (Advameg, Inc., http://www.referencefor-business.com/management/Mar-No/New-Product-Development.html, accessed January 12, 2011).

Thomas Morva, "Business to Business Marketing: An Introduction" (*EzineArticles*, http://ezinearticles.com/?Business-To-Business-Marketing:-An-Introduction&id=407951, accessed January 10, 2011).

Howard R. Moskowitz, Sebastiono Porretta, and Matthias Silcher, "Concept Research in Food Product Design and Development" (Ames, Iowa: Blackwell, 2005).

Debra Murphy, "Marketing for B2B vs. B2C—Similar but Different" (*Marketing Coach*, April 6, 2007, http://masterful-marketing.com/marketing-b2b-vs-b2c).

"New Product Failure Rates" (McDonough School of Business Faculty Index, http://faculty.msb.edu/homak/homahelpsite/webhelp/HomaHelp.htm#New_Product_Failure_Rates.htm, accessed January 12, 2011).

Camille Nicita and Christi Walters, "Blueprints to Successful Concept Development," in *Quirk's Marketing Research Review* (Quirk Enterprises, Inc., 2003).

Camille Nicita and Christi Walters, "Hearing the Customer's Voice," in *Quirk's Marketing Research Review* (2000).

Alex Pham, "Amazon Is Ready to Jump into the Next Chapter with Its Kindle" (*Cleveland.com*, January 8, 2011, http://www.cleveland.com/business/index.ssf/2011/01/amazons_vision_for_the_kindle.html, accessed January 18, 2011).

"What Is Qualitative Research?" (Qualitative Research Consultants Association, http://www.qrca.org/displaycommon.cfm?an=1&subarticlenbr=6, accessed November 3, 2010).

Ken Zino, "Volvo Cars Makes Bold Safety Claim: Zero" (*The Detroit Bureau*, September 25, 2009, http://www.thedetroitbureau.com/2009/09/volvo-cars-makes-bold-safety-claim-zero, accessed January 25, 2011).

ABOUT THE AUTHOR

Martha Guidry is the principal at The Rite Concept, based in Avon, Connecticut. The Rite Concept uses a flexible combination of qualitatively driven consumer understanding, hands-on learning, and ideation to help clients develop and optimize concepts for market. Martha brings more than 15 years of combined brand management, concept development, and research experience to each of her projects. After completing her MBA at Harvard, Martha spent 6 years in consumer marketing for Procter & Gamble and Hasbro Toys, prior to starting her own company

Clients perceive Martha as an unusually dynamic, creative, and resourceful consultant with the business know-how to drive their businesses to winning results. She can provide anything from a "complete package"—ideation through concept development—to a specific investigation into one particular part of the development process. Martha's work has spanned a variety of product and service categories. Her diverse client base includes Arby's, Pizza Hut, Dial (Henkel), Bush Beans, ShopRite Food Stores, Rug Doctor, The Hartford, DuPont, Amway and Fujifilm.

Martha gives back to the industry and her community in a variety of capacities. She is:

- A past director of the board for the Qualitative Research Consultants Association (QRCA), the American Marketing Association-CT chapter; and currently serves on the board of the Warner Theatre for the performing arts.
- A featured speaker at the QRCA National Conference and chapter meetings and at the Connecticut Business Expo.
- A published author in various marketing research publications (Quirk's Marketing Research Review, the AMA *Marketing News*, and *QRCA Views*).
- A committed volunteer with Safe Passage (an organization focused on breaking the cycle of poverty in Guatemala City), a teacher and marketing consultant at a local church, a middle school volleyball coach, and a fund-raiser for local initiatives.

Quickly and Efficiently Evaluate Concepts in Qualitative Research

Uniquely shaped, reusable plastic cards in the colors of a traffic light*

* Green = Yes/go
  Yellow = Maybe/caution
  Red = No/stop

- Understand target audience's intial reaction to concepts or other stimuli for further probing

- Easily show the clients in back-room how consumers feel about their ideas

- Helps minimize negative comments from influencing individuals who feel more positively about an concept or idea

- Works with all ages (children through seniors) and in any language

- Easy to use with single ring conveniently connecting all three cards together

nd out more information or purchase a set of 8 for your next project at

www.YesMaybeNoCards.com

CPSIA information can be obtained at www.ICGtesting.com
Printed in the USA
BVOW071937260712

296304BV00001B/2/P